P9-CDD-631

CRAFTSMAN BUNGALOWS

59 Homes from *The Craftsman*

Edited by
GUSTAV STICKLEY

New Introduction by
ALAN WEISSMAN

DOVER PUBLICATIONS, INC., NEW YORK

PUBLISHER'S NOTE

Readers interested in Craftsman-style bungalows should also consult the contents of Stickley's *Craftsman Homes* and *More Craftsman Homes* (Dover reprints 23791-5 and 24252-8, respectively). There is no duplication between the present collection, which gathers in one place the majority of the remaining *Craftsman* articles on bungalows, and the above-mentioned volumes.

Copyright ©1988 by Dover Publications, Inc.
All rights reserved under Pan American and International Copyright Conventions.

Published in Canada by General Publishing Company, Ltd., 30 Lesmill Road, Don Mills, Toronto, Ontario.
Published in the United Kingdom by Constable and Company, Ltd.

Craftsman Bungalows: 59 Homes from "The Craftsman," first published in 1988, is a new selection of 36 articles from the periodical *The Craftsman*, edited by Gustav Stickley, and originally published monthly from 1901 through 1916. The range of the present selection is from December 1903 to August 1916 (the date of each article appears in the Table of Contents). The contents of the articles are unabridged, but for reasons of space the format has in some cases been slightly altered. A new introduction has been written for this edition by Alan Weissman.

Manufactured in the United States of America
Dover Publications, Inc., 31 East 2nd Street, Mineola, N.Y. 11501

Library of Congress Cataloging-in-Publication Data

Craftsman bungalows and small homes : 59 homes from the Craftsman / edited by Gustav Stickley.
      p.   cm.
    Reprint of 36 articles from the periodical the Craftsman, originally published from Dec. 1903 to Aug. 1916, with a new introduction by Alan Weissman.
    ISBN 0-486-25829-7 (pbk.)
    1. Bungalows—United States. 2. Small houses—United States. 3. Craftsman (Eastwood, Syracuse, N.Y.) I. Stickley, Gustav, 1858–1942.
NA7571.C76 1988
728.3'73—dc19   88-23772
                                             CIP

INTRODUCTION TO THE DOVER EDITION

THE CRAFTSMAN STYLE of early twentieth-century residential architecture was the result of many convergent tendencies: the rise of the middle class; the proliferation of the democratic ideal; the increase in individual home ownership; a growing interest in nature and "natural living"; and the American Arts and Crafts movement, which recognized and adapted itself to all of these tendencies.

The Arts and Crafts movement, begun in nineteenth-century England by such artists and philosopher-critics as John Ruskin and, especially, William Morris, rejected modern machine-produced artifacts as unaesthetic and much academic art and architecture, based mainly on the perpetuation of traditional, highly artificial styles, as out of harmony with actual modern living. The Arts and Crafts ideal was, as the name implies, the union of the fine and decorative arts, which, it was claimed, were essentially one in the first place. The natural form of what is truly shaped to human needs by individual craftsmanship was considered to constitute real beauty in an artifact or work of architecture. At least originally, medieval craftsmanship (but not slavish adherence to medieval forms) was taken as a standard by Morris and his followers.

The major voice of the Arts and Crafts movement in the United States was Gustav Stickley (1858–1942), furniture maker, architect, and editor of *The Craftsman* (1901–1916). This monthly magazine was begun as the journal of the United Crafts of Eastwood, New York, a guild of furniture makers founded by Stickley on William Morris' principles. Because of the Craftsman philosophy of the unity of all arts and crafts, and their inseparability from the needs of actual social life, *The Craftsman* from the first published articles not merely on Craftsman furniture but also on various handicrafts, on modern social and economic conditions, on the history of the medieval guilds, and on the lives of Morris, Ruskin, and other inspirers of the Arts and Crafts movement. The items of furniture hand-produced by the United Craftsmen were conceived of as fitting integrally into the houses for which they were intended. A natural consequence is that increased attention began to be paid to the designing of houses. Soon an ideal of the "Craftsman House" began to evolve, and more space in *The Craftsman* was devoted to plans and descriptions of houses.

In 1904, Gustav Stickley visited California and was taken with the grand simplicity of the old Spanish missions and their harmony with their surroundings. Thenceforward the Mission style became part of the Craftsman ideal, although "Mission" and "Craftsman" were never synonymous terms, as many today erroneously believe. Indeed, Stickley inveighed against manufacturers of shabbily constructed furniture glamorized by the phony label "Mission." Many Craftsman homes did show a strong California-mission influence. Others, however, were utterly unlike the California or any other mission. The important thing was that the house be in harmony with its environment, as the wooden house in the treeless desert and the adobe house in the forest manifestly were not.

The idea that a human habitation should harmonize with its surroundings accounts for the large number of *Craftsman* articles on gardens and nature and for the fact that so many Craftsman houses had porches and pergolas as a means of unifying life indoors and outdoors. Again, California's climate was ideal for such a lifestyle, but Craftsman houses were also adapted to places as diverse as Michigan, New Jersey, and even New Zealand.

Many, perhaps most, of the houses featured in *The Craftsman* were not actually designed by Stickley or his associates. Rather, *The Craftsman* would report on examples of houses that exemplified its goals. Or else, the owners or architects of new houses, having been influenced by the philosophy and practical home-designing suggestions printed in *The Craftsman*, gratefully furnished plans and descriptions of their residences to Stickley's magazine, and Stickley in turn was glad to print these embodiments of the Craftsman spirit for the further inspiration they might provide.

Harmony of life indoors was as important to Stickley as that between the house and its setting. Wherever possible, furnishings such as cabinets, sideboards, benches, and bookshelves were built in as integral components of the rooms. Communal living spaces were unified, avoiding the hitherto-prevalent compartmentalization of rooms. A view of the living-room space from the adjoining dining area was considered an aesthetic enhancement to the latter, and vice versa, and the sense of spaciousness was a further step away from the stuffiness of the typical Victorian house. A fireplace—essential to Craftsman houses, even in Southern California—served to draw the family together and was a sort of social center to every Craftsman residence.

The Craftsman idea was broad enough to include farmhouses, suburban houses, mountain cabins, and semidetached city houses. There were Craftsman mansions and Craftsman cottages. The important thing was suitability—suitability of occupants to house and of house to surroundings. Over the sixteen-year span of *The Craftsman*, however, one style of dwelling did come to receive more attention than any other: the bungalow.

The word "bungalow," from the Hindi *baṅglā*, or house in the Bengal style, originally referred to a type of colonial dwelling in East India. This was a single-story house whose well-ventilated rooms opened off a central airy hall, and which had a low-pitched roof and a verandah on all sides. For a time a form of the bungalow became fashionable in England. In the early twentieth century, the American Arts and Crafts movement unofficially adopted it as the ideal Craftsman house. In practice the Craftsman bungalow departed considerably from the original Indian model. There were even two-story bungalows. But especially in Southern California, a region for which the bungalow was ideally suited, the original spirit prevailed, insofar as the mild climate permitted a more thorough integration of the house with its immediate surroundings than would have been possible elsewhere. The dining room, for example, might open onto a closed porch, which would adjoin a patio or garden; or bedrooms would adjoin a sleeping porch. No matter what the size of the house, there would be at least one porch. For the sake of both economy and a sense of coziness, ceilings were usually low. Windows were usually abundant, and the bungalow incorporated all the other features considered essential to the Craftsman ideal. What was considered an excess of ornamentation was kept to a minimum, and an abundance of halls, passageways, and stairways avoided. As in all Craftsman homes, beauty would arise from the natural function of simple forms inherent in the structure, from the natural appearance of the fine materials used, and from the high standards of craftsmanship uniformly applied. The sense of unity with the surroundings was maintained at least partly by using locally available construction materials.

Ideally, and in many actual instances reported in *The Craftsman*, the owner-occupant of a Craftsman bungalow had participated personally in every stage of its design and construction. Many bungalows were modest habitations affordable by those of exceedingly modest means. And, in equal adherence to a democratic ideal, the wealthy owner of a more sizable "bungalow" was expected to devote personal labor—not just money—toward making the dwelling conform to his or her individual needs. High standards of craftsmanship and hard work, not needless expense and elaborate ornamentation, were the essentials.

The approximately five dozen bungalows depicted or discussed in the following 36 articles from *The Craftsman* in the years 1903 through 1916 are of many different types but they all embody Stickley's ideals. Gustav Stickley was not a radically innovative architect like Frank Lloyd Wright, but his architectural philosophy, founded on his own views of the importance of the environmental, social, even ethical *gestalt*, had its own influence. His professed wish was "that the Craftsman house may . . . be instrumental in helping to establish in America a higher ideal, not only of beautiful architecture, but of home life." That he at least partly succeeded in his aim is evidenced by the lasting presence throughout the United States of many Craftsman-style houses. Greatly sought-after by those who can afford them at today's prices, these unpretentious but naturally elegant dwellings, whether in urban, suburban, or rural surroundings, are among the best-constructed and at the same time most comfortable residences of any period that still stand in America.

ALAN WEISSMAN

TABLE OF CONTENTS

How to Build a Bungalow

The term "Bungalow" in the process of transplantation from the banks of the Ganges to the shores of Saranac Lake and other summer abiding places, has lost its significance in a large measure; the American bungalow being nothing more or less than a summer residence of extreme simplicity, of economic construction and intended for more or less primitive living. In too many instances the summer residence, in spite of the every appeal from the woods, the streams and the rocks for simplicity, is but an illy-designed suburban house taken bodily, in many instances, from architectural pattern books.

In response to many requests The Craftsman presents herewith various drawings in which it is intended to give a solution of the problem. The exterior presents a combination of materials easily obtainable in any locality, which may be put together by any man having the slightest knowledge of mason-work and carpentry. The building is constructed in the usual manner of the balloon framed houses, covered with sheathing tarred paper, over which are placed large pine, cedar, or red-wood shingles, as are most available in the locality in which the building is situated. It is purposed to stain these shingles a dull burnt sienna color, and the roof in a color technically known as silver-stain. This

1

ELEVATION OF FRONT

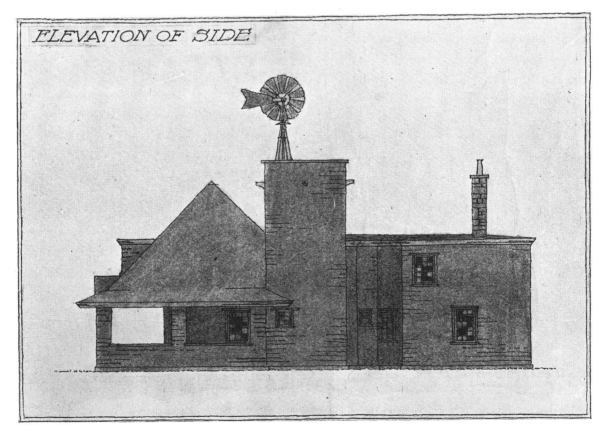

ELEVATION OF SIDE

sienna color, in a very short time, comes to look like an autumn oak leaf; and this, together with the rough stone of the large chimney, tends to tie the building to its surroundings and to give it the seeming of a growth rather than of a creation. It is a curious fact that the principles laid down by the late lamented Frederick Law Olmsted, relative to the coloration of buildings with regard to their surroundings,—principles so capable of demonstration and so obvious,—should meet with so little recognition; and that, instead of structures which seem to grow from the plain or the forest and become a part of the landscape, we have otherwise admirable architectural efforts that affront the sensitive eye; crying aloud in white lead and yellow ochre the blindness of the owner to even the A B C of decorative fitness. The large and spacious veranda, the simple forms of the roof, and the short distances between joints (eight feet, six inches) tend to give the construction an air of genuine homeliness: a quality in design much to be sought for and not always attained. It is, however, a subject for congratulation that the country side is no longer affronted with lean, narrow, two-story houses surmounted by mansard roofs, and situated on farms of anywhere from seventy-five to two hundred acres; the designers of these monstrosities seeming to have forgotten that the mansard roof was the result of the endeavor to evade the building laws of Paris, and equally seeming to be unconscious of the fact that the building laws on the average farm are not quite so stringent.

The interior is as simple as the outside, and while presenting no particular novelty of plan or construction, is deemed worthy of consideration. In order that the sylvan note may be retained equally as in the outside, the interior, as far as its color is concerned, aspires to harmonize with the dull but rich tones of autumnal oak leaves. This quality, which is only too often neglected, should be strongly insisted upon in all structures of this nature, as it is not easy of accomplishment to be in touch with Nature and at the same time to live in an environment of white and gold, accented with Louis XV. furniture.

The large general living room, with an ample fire-place and the bookcase for the few necessary volumes of summer reading, together with the other features indicated by the perspective drawing, gives it a certain distinction that is oftentimes lacking in erections of this class. The walls of this room are sheathed and covered with burlap of a dull olive yellow, while the exposed construction of the ceiling is stained a wet mossy green color, by a mixture, which, while inappropriate to side walls, seems on the ceiling, where it may not be handled, to serve the purpose better than anything else. Water color tempered with glycerine, —the glycerine never drying as oils would do,—in this instance serves the purpose very much better and gives to the color incorporated in it a suggestion of the woodland to be obtained in no other manner. The floor is of hard maple, and will receive a dark shade of brown, considerably lower in value than any other color in the room. The balance of the woodwork throughout the house is preferably of cypress; but should contingencies require, it may be of hemlock. The visible stone-work of the fireplace (if it can be obtained), will be of limestone that has weathered by exposure a

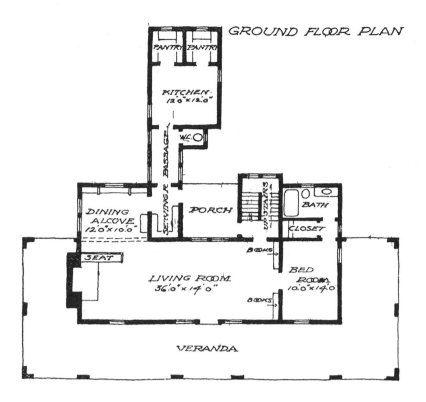

GROUND FLOOR PLAN

PANTRY PANTRY

KITCHEN
12'0"x12'0"

SERVING PASSAGE

W.C.

DINING
ALCOVE
12'0"x10'0"

PORCH

UPSTAIRS

BATH

CLOSET

BOOKS

SEAT

LIVING ROOM
36'0"x14'0"

BED
ROOM
10'0"x14'0"

BOOKS

VERANDA

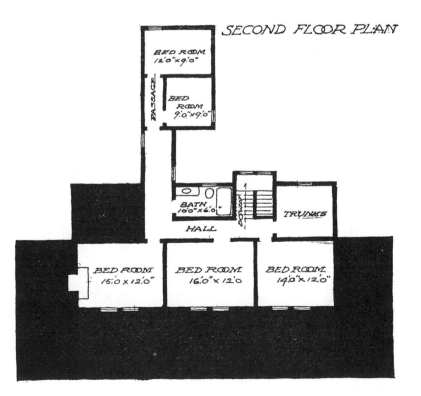

SECOND FLOOR PLAN

BED ROOM
12'0"x9'0"

PASSAGE

BED
ROOM
9'0"x9'0"

BATH
10'0"x6'0"

DOWN

TRUNKS

HALL

BED ROOM
15'0"x12'0"

BED ROOM
16'0"x12'0"

BED ROOM
14'0"x12'0"

5

sufficient length of time to give it that characteristic spongy look found in the strippings of limestone quarries. This treatment, if used with raked-out joints, is extremely effective and will harmonize admirably with the simplicity of the plans of the house, and, at the same time, give a strong masculine note. From the height of the top of the door to the underside of the ceiling extends a frieze in stencil, of conventional objects relating to primitive life, done in the same straight-forward manner as the balance of the structure. In this decoration the slightest attempt at anything beyond pure symbolism would result in disaster, as the building is essentially primitive in its general design, and equally so should be the decoration. This arrangement, together with window hangings of extreme simplicity, such as a figured creton in varying shades of pale yellow accented with dull red, should satisfactorily complete the room.

The dining-alcove, opening from this apartment, being a continuation of the living room, is treated in the same manner. The permanent fittings of the alcove consist of a primitive sideboard and a convenient and unobtrusive serving shelf.

The alcove, separated from the living room by the arch and two posts, as indicated in the drawing, is so arranged that it may be used either as a portion of the living room, or as a provision for guests, as a bedchamber. It is provided with a couch, which may serve as a bed, a chest of drawers, a pier glass and a writing desk; the pier glass facing the large fireplace in the living room and reflecting the same. The kitchen, and its accompanying offices, are, as this bungalow is intended for summer occupation only, semi-detached and only connected by means of a covered way, from which, except in inclement weather, the glass and sash are removed. For obvious reasons the cellarage for the kitchen is omitted and such storage as is desired is provided for on the ground floor. The bed rooms are moderately spacious and easy of ventilation. The treatment of the bed room, as far as material and color are concerned, is identical with that of the living room: viz., burlap side walls and stained construction of the ceiling; the former of olive green; the latter of moss green.

The sanitary arrangements of the bungalow consist of a single bath room on the second story, supplied with a tub and an earth closet, together with a lavatory on the ground floor; and the provisions for water are made by the wind-mill shown.

In connection with these drawings is a scheme which, for the usual site in which this bungalow would be built, seems adequate, proper, and tending to unite the structure to its surroundings without the usual abrupt transition from handicraft to Nature.

THE BUNGALOW'S FURNITURE

If, after having been built with great respect for harmony and appropriateness, the bungalow should be filled with the usual collection of badly designed and inadequate furniture, the *ensemble* would be distressing, and the thought involved in the structure of the building thrown away. The term furniture implies, *per se*, movable portions of the building, and, as such, should be conceived by the designer. Otherwise, nine times out of ten, an unpleasant sense of incongruity prevails. The importance of

Fireplace in living room

Alcove off of living room

7

unity between the furniture and the structure, in spite of the fact that every writer on the topic has insisted upon it, in the majority of instances is further from realization than it was in the Stone Age, when, by force of circumstances, harmony of manners, methods and materials was a necessity. It is not intended by this to suggest that we should return to that period, but to emphasize the fact that necessity involves simplicity and that simplicity is the key note of harmony. This furniture, while adapted with much precision to its various functions, is of almost primitive directness. It is done in oak with a pale olive Craftsman finish, and thus becomes an integral part of the bungalow.

Whatever hardware is used in connection with this furniture is of wrought-iron, in the "Russian finish," which falls into place very readily in the general scheme.

Great care has been taken in furnishing this bungalow to omit every article that is not absolutely essential to the comfort or the convenience of the occupants, it not being intended to make the building in a small way a cheap museum to be indifferently managed by an amateur curator, as is usually the case in urban residences and frequently happens in the summer cottage, to the great disturbance of the simple life.

A FOREST BUNGALOW

WORDS themselves, like the thoughts of which they are the winged messengers, modify their meaning, as they pass from mouth to mouth. Formerly, the name Bungalow, when pronounced, reflected in the minds of those who heard it pic-

Front elevation

tures of the East Indies. And to those who were unable to represent to themselves the suburbs of Bombay or Calcutta, the dictionaries offered the following definition:

"Bungalow,—a house or cottage of a single story, with a tiled or thatched roof."

Such definition is no longer adequate. The idea of the convenient little habitation has developed and extended during its passage to new countries. The single story and thatch, or tiles, are no longer the essentials of the Bungalow. Camps or cottages passing under this name, and in which the primitive type native to British India is wholly obscured, accent the Atlantic coast, the Adirondack forests, and the shores of the Saint

Lawrence. A structure of the later, more advanced type, as may be learned by reference to the accompanying illustrations, is now offered by The Craftsman, in response to the demands of the vacation period.

The Bungalow here presented in elevation, is designed to be set low, with the first floor at a level not exceeding eight inches above the surrounding grade.

The building is supported by rough piers of masonry extending below the frost line; while the pillars upholding the roof are tree trunks, still covered with their bark.

The structural timber employed is hemlock or spruce, rough from the mill; the frame being covered with matched boards, surfaced on

Side elevation

the inner side. This boarding may be overlaid on the outer side with building paper, in order to assure additional warmth, and the walls are lastly covered with split shingles, laid wide to the weather and left to acquire a natural stain. The large area of the roof with its dormers, is also covered by shingles; in this instance of the ordinary kind; brush-coated to a deep moss-green.

A Forest Bungalow

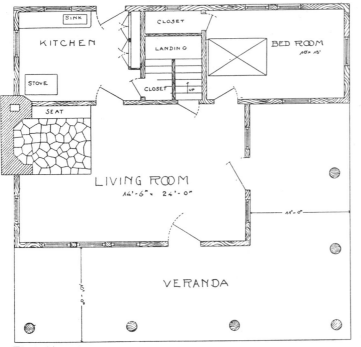

First floor plan

is left exposed with the intervening panels either stained to a warm brown, or hung with burlap, as desired. The ceiling is not covered: the exposed floor-joists of the second story thus giving it a beamed effect.

A cross-section at the rear of the building contains, at the right: a bedroom, ten by fifteen feet in size, with dependent closet; next, an ample space is devoted to the staircase which opens into the living room; while the large square remaining at the left of the rear cross-section, forms a well-ventilated, convenient kitchen, provided with a built-in cupboard, a sink with drain-board, and a second cupboard or closet made by utilizing the space beneath the stairs.

The batten doors can easily be made upon the site; the flooring of the veranda is of two-inch plank; the chimney is built of boulders gathered from the locality, with field stones used as binders to strengthen the masonry.

The space of the first floor is apportioned into a living room, a bed room and a kitchen.

The first of these rooms has dimensions of fourteen feet, six inches by twenty-four feet; one end being occupied by a fire-place large enough to contain a four foot log. The hearth is formed of large flat stones set in a bed of earth, and the floor of the room is laid in matched pine boards, six inches in width. The studding of the side walls

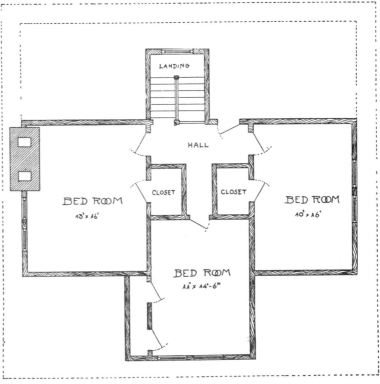

Second floor plan

The second floor contains three bedrooms, with storage room under the eaves at the rear of the building: this extension of space being in itself a proof that the Bungalow, in its later development, is a habitation much more convenient and agreeable than existed in its primitive form.

THE CALIFORNIA BUNGALOW: A STYLE OF ARCHITECTURE WHICH EXPRESSES THE INDIVIDUALITY AND FREEDOM CHARACTERISTIC OF OUR WESTERN COAST

WE have the pleasure of publishing in this issue of THE CRAFTSMAN some of the best examples that have come to us of the new American architecture, which as yet can hardly be considered a style so much as a series of individual plans adapted to climatic conditions and to the needs of daily living, and in harmony with the natural environment and contour of the landscape. In a country like our own, where all these requirements vary so widely, any one style would be altogether inadequate, but the new architecture that is so rapidly and steadily developing in America is rather a general expression of that spirit of individuality and freedom which is especially characteristic of this country. In the north and east, for example, a style of building is required which would be absolutely out of harmony with the life and surroundings to be found in the south and west, and in California,— especially in the southern part of the state,—conditions prevail which are found hardly anywhere else on the continent. For fully eight months in the year the constant sunshine, unbroken by clouds or storms and relieved only by an occasional fog drifting in from the ocean, permits a life that is practically all out-of-doors, or, at all events, maintains such a friendly relation with out-of-doors that the house seems more in the nature of a temporary shelter and resting place than a building designed to be lived in all the time and to afford constant protection from the elements.

The country out there is one of great restful spaces, with wide plains and low, rolling hills which lead up gradually to the stupendous mountain walls of the Sierra Nevada and the lesser but still imposing peaks of the Coast Range and the Sierra Madre. There are no thickets of slim saplings and green undergrowth, no little creeks and springs, and none of the somewhat aggressive picturesqueness found at every hand in the east; only huge grain fields, orchards and vineyards and wide stretches of sun-dried grass, scorched to a warm, tawny brown during the long rainless season that follows the brief winter of green grass and wild flowers. The colors, too, are differ-

Residence for Mr. Robt. C. Gillis.
Myron Hunt & Elmer Grey, Archts.
Los Angeles, Calif.

"THE ADOBE WALLS, WHICH WERE FORMERLY BUILT FOR DEFENSE, ARE NOW MODIFIED INTO GARDEN WALLS, WHICH AFFORD COMPLETE SECLUSION.

A California House and Garden

Myron Hunt & Elmer Grey, Archts.

"THERE ARE HALF-COVERED PORCHES (PERGOLAS) THAT SUGGEST SHADE AND COOL, AND STILL ALLOW THE SUN TO CARPET THE GROUND WITH DAPPLED SHADOWS."

HOUSE & GARDEN for DR. GUY COCHRAN

MYRON HUNT & ELMER GREY, ARCHITECTS, LOS ANGELES, CAL.

"THE GROUPING OF THE WINDOWS IS A FEATURE OF MARKED INDIVIDUALITY: THEY DO AWAY WITH THE SENSE OF BEING ENCLOSED WITHIN WALLS."

15

Residence for Pasadena Calif.
Myron Hunt & Elmer Grey, Architects
Los Angeles.

"IN A COUNTRY WITH THE CONTOUR AND COLOR-
ING OF CALIFORNIA THERE CAN BE NO STYLE
OF ARCHITECTURE SO HARMONIOUS AS THAT
FOUNDED UPON THE OLD MISSION BUILDINGS."

ent. Our watery, gray-blue skies and the blue haze of the distance is replaced by burning sapphire overhead and an atmosphere so filled with the golden dust haze that all distance disappears in a mist of warm rosy violet.

In a country with the contour and coloring of Southern California there can be no style of architecture so harmonious as that founded directly upon the old Mission buildings, and no material that blends so beautifully with the colors about it as some modification of the old adobe or sun-dried brick, covered with creamy plaster. The old Mission padres knew what they were about, and in nothing that remains of their work is this knowledge more convincingly shown than in the plans of the old Mission buildings which were the forerunners of the modern adobe houses. Even the adobe walls, which were formerly erected for defence against hostile Indians outside the Mission grounds and the protection not only of the monks but of the Mission Indians who sought refuge within the enclosures, are now modified into garden walls which afford complete seclusion, if desired, by giving a garden close, filled with green grass and tropical foliage, which is almost a part of the house.

Messrs. Myron Hunt and Elmer Grey, the architects who designed the houses shown here, are pioneers in the development of the new American architecture. They both brought to their work in Southern California the energy and progressive spirit of the Middle West and the training of finished architects. Mr. Hunt went to Los Angeles from Chicago and Mr. Grey from Milwaukee, both in search of the improved health that is to be found in the mild and equable climate of Southern California, and in going out there both found the ideal conditions for the full development of a very unusual gift for designing simple and beautiful buildings, which are also remarkable examples of direct thought based on the fundamental principle of response to need. As Mr. Grey says:

"Many eastern people seem to consider that we have a distinctive style out here. If such a quality does exist in California architecture, it is not because our architects have striven to be unique in their designing, but because they have tried to eliminate from it all features not properly belonging to their climate and to their local conditions,—because they have tried to be simply natural. The California architect is not surrounded, as is the easterner, by a great mass of previously constructed buildings, constituting a dead weight of tradition from which it is difficult to break away; he is in a comparatively new country, the climate of which is radically different from other portions of the United States, and so in design he seeks suggestion, not from the work about him,—which is apt like his own to be more or less experimental,—nor from remote parts of the country which are very different from this; but from Italy, Spain or Mexico, where similar climatic conditions prevail. If he has a proper sense of the fitness of things he will not implant amid the semi-tropical foliage of California such architecture, for instance, as the Queen Anne or the Elizabethan. He may admire the English style greatly, and may have profited by some of its lessons, but if his designs show anything of this influence they will also express his loyalty to California and his desire not to place any foreign element in

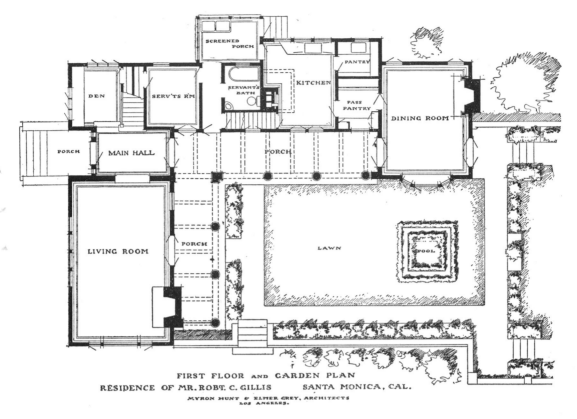

FIRST FLOOR AND GARDEN PLAN
RESIDENCE OF MR. ROBT. C. GILLIS   SANTA MONICA, CAL.
MYRON HUNT & ELMER GREY, ARCHITECTS
LOS ANGELES.

it that has not first been thoroughly naturalized. His respect for traditional architecture may be profound; but because he does not wish to see destroyed what little tradition his own part of the country may have, he feels bound to respect its peculiarities and to try to preserve its architectural integrity in his work."

The examples shown here amply illustrate the viewpoint held by Mr. Grey. They are almost all planned after the manner of the bungalow, a word which is generally used to convey the idea of a dwelling with its rooms all on the ground floor. Such a house, of course, is not well adapted to a cold climate, as it is difficult to heat easily and economically a number of rooms spread over the ground. In California this objection has no weight, as there is no need of heating any house save by means of an occasional fireplace, and the bungalow there has the advantage of simplifying housekeeping and making its occupants feel a closer relationship to the great out-of-doors. The California bungalow does not, however, resemble the original East Indian dwelling of that name so closely as it does the old Mexican *hacienda* or ranch house, which was almost invariably built around three and sometimes four sides of a square or rectangular court. This style is called a *patio* house, and it makes a most delightful form of dwelling for Southern California. Such a house, of course, must be surrounded by trees and spacious grounds, as it would be entirely out of place in a city lot with high buildings around it, and

THE CALIFORNIA BUNGALOW

so again it conforms to the conditions of life in Southern California rather than to those of the east.

THE dwelling of Mr. Robert C. Gillis, although a decided modification of the *patio* house, is a characteristic example of a house intended for life in Southern California. The garden is enclosed within a wall which affords a sense of privacy from the street without giving any feeling of confinement or separation from the country all around. The living room opens directly upon the long porch, from which one again walks out almost on the same level onto the lawn. The only way to reach the dining room is through the porch which runs at right angles to that opening from the living room. The entrance to the house is on the opposite side from this porch, and one especially attractive feature of the plan is the long vista across the main hall and porch through the dining room and along the entire length of the gar-

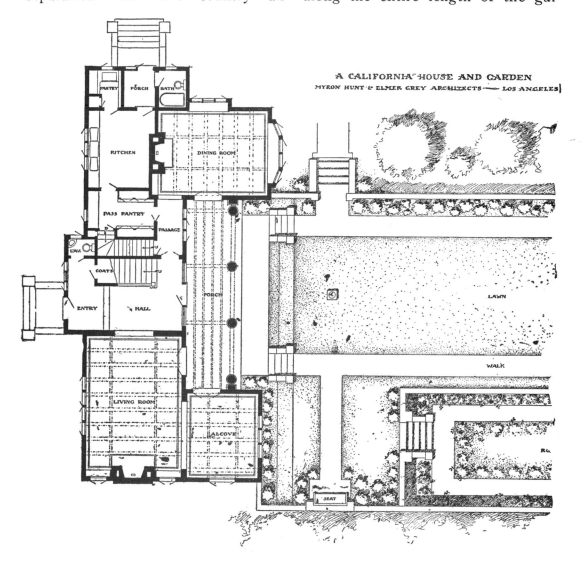

A CALIFORNIA HOUSE AND GARDEN
MYRON HUNT & ELMER GREY ARCHITECTS — LOS ANGELES

THE CALIFORNIA BUNGALOW

den. French windows are employed in the place of doors, so that nothing occurs to break the vista. The main bedrooms are all upstairs facing the court.

IN the design called "A California House and Garden," a still greater departure from the strict form of the *patio* house and a nearer approach to the more usual eastern planning is seen, yet the principal features of this house plainly show its adaptation to the California environment. The dining room is approached most easily from the living room by way of the covered porch, the small pas-

sage between the hall and the dining room being incorporated merely as an emergency thoroughfare to be used in inclement weather. Here again a delightful vista, through glass doors and windows across the porch and then down the length of the garden, is seen by anyone entering the hall. Both the living room and dining room face the garden, while the kitchen is placed upon the north side of the house facing the street, so that the main outlook is always upon the beauty and seclusion of the enclosure that is dedicated as the house itself to the family life. One feature of this

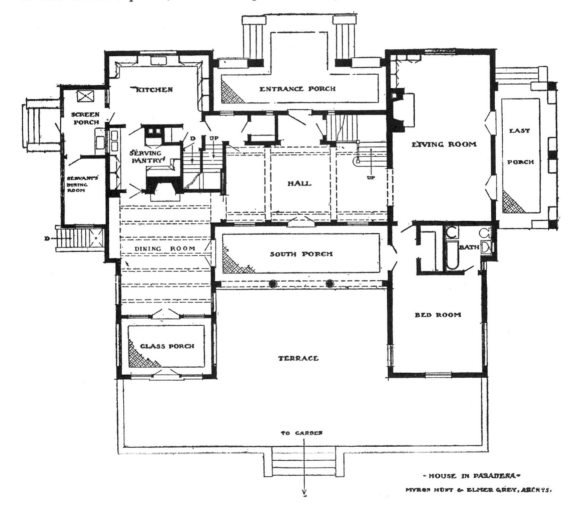

- HOUSE IN PASADENA -
MYRON HUNT & ELMER GREY, ARCHTS.

THE CALIFORNIA BUNGALOW

house that adds much to its attractive individuality is the grouping of the windows, which not only admit the greatest possible amount of air and sunshine, but form an admirable division of the wall space. The bedrooms are all upstairs facing the garden, which, of course, is the sunny side of the house.

THE chance to live out of doors Pasadena shows less of an enclosure within the walls of the house and a larger enclosed space out of doors, the whole plan of the garden being such that the house is merely the center of a well-balanced scheme.

The entrance porch is on the north side of the house, and directly across the large hall is the south porch which leads out to the broad terrace, from which steps go down into the garden. The living room opens upon the east porch and the dining room is a closed porch at the south side which connects directly with the terrace. All the bedrooms, save one, are upstairs, and a beautiful feature of the second story is the pergola covered with vines, which affords a charming outdoor sitting room that is shaded with green and yet cuts off very little light and no air from the bedrooms.

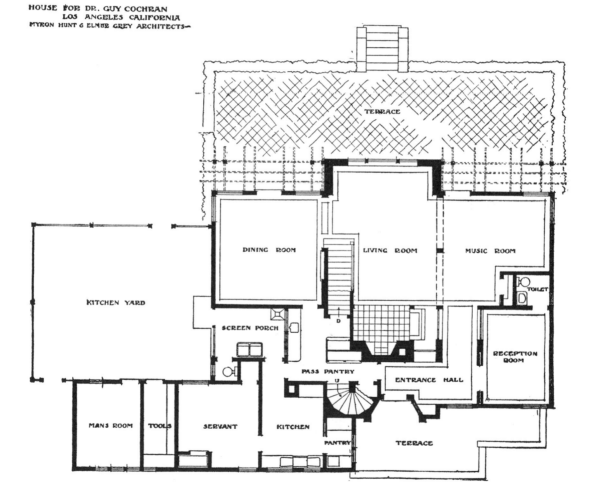

HOUSE FOR DR. GUY COCHRAN
LOS ANGELES CALIFORNIA
MYRON HUNT & ELMER GREY ARCHITECTS

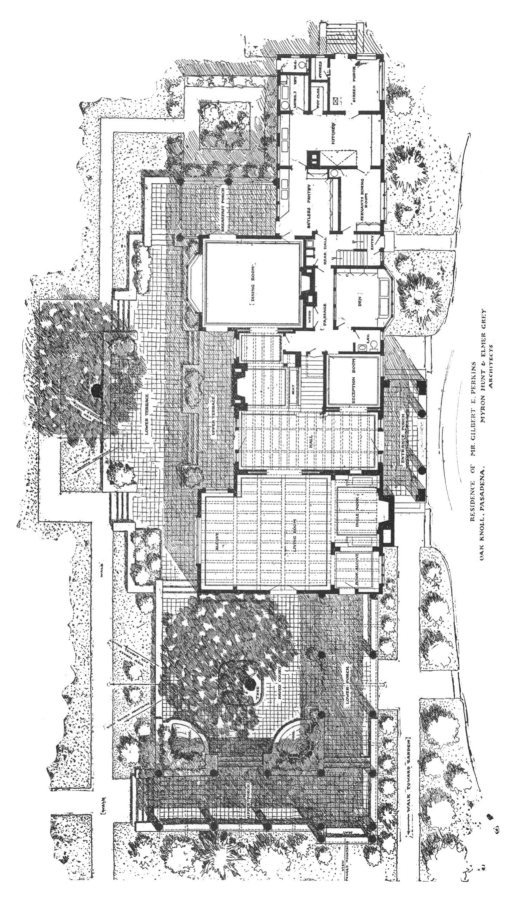

RESIDENCE OF MR. GILBERT E. PERKINS
OAK KNOLL, PASADENA.
MYRON HUNT & ELMER GREY
ARCHITECTS

THE CALIFORNIA BUNGALOW

*Porch and Terrace — The Gilbert E. Perkins Residence
Mayers Hunt — Elmer Grey, Architects.*

The beautiful lines and proportions of this house and its perfect suitability to its surroundings make it one of the best examples of the group.

PERHAPS the very best, though, is the house and garden designed for Dr. Guy Cochran, which is less distinctively Californian in design, but is nevertheless admirably adapted for the southern climate and outdoor life, and in itself is one of the most beautiful houses which has ever been reproduced in the pages of THE CRAFTSMAN. Here again the grouping of the windows is a feature of such marked individuality that it commands the attention with the first look at the house. The enormous windows from the living room, looking out upon the terrace and garden, give such a sense of relationship between the two that there is almost no feeling of being enclosed within walls. The French windows seen elsewhere give the same sense of direct communication with the garden from the dining room and the music room, and equally large casements placed just above look out from the upper rooms upon the green drapery of the two pergolas that shade the terrace. The long line of casements shown in the broad, low dormer that seems to grow out of the roof gives exactly the right balance to the great spread of glass below, and the lines of the roof itself are so friendly, gracious and inviting in their suggestion of comfort and shelter that they add the last touch of the feeling of inevitableness that is conveyed by the whole design. Here again the garden is almost a part of the house and is walled away from the street on one side and the cliff on the other.

ONLY a suggestion is given in the small line drawings made of "Oak Knoll," Mr. Gilbert Perkins' residence in Pasadena, but the large floor plan showing the way in which

THE CALIFORNIA BUNGALOW

the house and garden are laid out and connected so closely that they may almost be called interwoven, gives a better idea of the beauty of this place than the most elaborately detailed perspective. When reduced to its essential elements the plan is quite simple. The main rooms of the first story are the living room, hall, dining room and kitchen, as the little reception room and den are merely incidents and can hardly be included as important parts of the plan. The unusual and most delightful feature of this house is the system of paved terraces built around two spreading live oak trees. One of these oaks at the side of the house is completely surrounded by a covered porch, the square or court thus formed being paved with tile and made delightfully attractive by a semi-formal arrangement of paths and steps leading up to the higher portion of the porch. The other oak is situated in front of the house and also has terraces built all around it, thus making additional living space which receives the benefit of its shade. From both of these terraces a magnificent view of the San Gabriel valley and of the Sierra Madre mountains is obtained. Although the interior plan of this house is not so very different from many eastern houses, the system of terraces and porches and the means provided for ready access to all of these is well worth studying as a plan that is admirably adapted to Southern California, as it is most expressive both

of the country and of the sunny, leisurely outdoor life that under all normal conditions is lived there by everyone.

THE chance to live out of doors and yet enjoy the utmost comfort, even luxury, is what the California bungalow suggests, not only at a first glimpse, but after most careful investigation. The entire building is kept close to the ground; there are groups of windows that bring indoors the pleasure of blue sky, of purple hills or wide stretches of hazy prairie; there are vine-covered pergolas that suggest shade and cool, and still leave patches of blue overhead and allow the sun to carpet the ground with dappled shadows of leaves and beams. The house, the garden, the terrace, the patio, the open porch are all one domain, one shelter from the outside world. It is home in that big, fine sense of the word that leaves the horizon, not four walls, for the boundary lines.

And this dwelling, which at the first blush seems but a cross between an East Indian bungalow and a Mission adobe house, in reality proves to be the most genuine expression of American feeling in domestic architecture that has yet appeared. Built to suit the needs of one great section of our country, it has developed a beauty and a charm of its own. It is original because it is like the country it has grown out of; it is becoming a definite style because it has met a definite demand, and because it is genuine it will be permanent.

24

A SMALL BUNGALOW WORTH STUDYING

ABOUT three and a half miles from Pasadena is located a bungalow, here illustrated, designed and built by Mr. Louis B. Easton for Mr. C. C. Curtis. The house 44 feet x 32 feet, and barn 20 feet by 80 feet, together form a ranch house, and the barn, built in the form of an "L," makes a court at the back and adds mass to the combined structure. At the rear, and within easy view, stands Mt. Lowe with its observatory, and running down the mountain the inclined road of the Pacific Electric. The house has the lines of the old Mexican buildings of adobe, but differs from them in construction, being built of boards running up and down and heavily battened. Such a bungalow, carefully built, would be entirely practical for an all-the-year-round home in California, and, where one wishes to live the simple life, is much better adapted to winter use in this locality than the regulation small house.

The central living room, 20 feet x 23 feet, has a big fireplace with a high settle at one side, which serves a double purpose. The back of this settle faces the entrance door, thus helping to form a vestibule and making a convenient place for hanging wraps and coats, while at the same time it shelters the fireplace from the wind.

At the opposite side of the fireplace is a built-in bookcase nine feet in length, beyond which are a desk and typewriter desk, furnished with a long bench upon which, when at work, one may easily move from one to the other. A couple of magazine racks, a rough table and a few chairs complete the furnishings of this room. In the dining room are a built-in buffet, a round table and old splint chairs, which lend an air of homely comfort and cheer.

All lumber throughout the house is of rough redwood, smoothed with a steel brush. The ceilings are of 14-inch boards battened on the upper side, and these, as well as the boarding on the outside of the buildings, are the color of weathered driftwood. Beams and trim are finished in a dark brown tone, with which the burlap above the wainscot is in harmony.

Provision is made for hot and cold water, the plumbing is much better than that which is provided in the usual five-room house, and under all is a good cellar.

Facing west, the house fronts on a beautiful lawn, with a young orchard at the north and a rose garden at the south. The bungalow as a whole seems simply to have found lodgment at the foot of a great mountain, where it makes no pretense beyond that of offering shelter and comfort.

See page 534

A BUNGALOW NEAR PASADENA DESIGNED BY
LOUIS B. EASTON, WHICH HAS THE LINES OF
THE OLD MISSION HOUSE, THOUGH BUILT OF
BOARDS.

LOOKING FROM DINING ROOM THROUGH SIT-
TING ROOM TO BEDROOM, SHOWING INTEREST-
ING INTERIOR CONSTRUCTION.

See page 534

VIEW OF SITTING ROOM IN BUNGALOW
DESIGNED FOR MR. C. C. CURTIS.

27

INTERESTING TIMBER CONSTRUCTION IN A CALIFORNIA BUNGALOW

THE bungalow shown in the accompanying illustration was designed by Mr. C. W. Buchanan for Mr. Furrows of Pasadena, California. It is interesting to note how closely the graceful proportions and structural effects of this little dwelling suggest the simplicity of the wooden temples of the early Greeks.

The roof has a projection of three feet at the eaves, which makes the building appear lower than it is. The timbers that support it are exposed, which relieves the

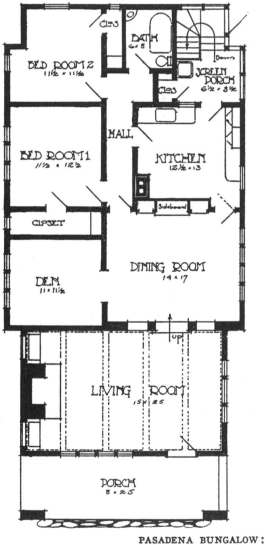

PASADENA BUNGALOW:
FLOOR PLAN.

long edges of the slopes and gives the keynote of sturdiness to the whole structure. The house is covered with 8-inch clapboards one inch thick, and the heavy shadows cast by their overlapping edges maintain, even from a distance, the rugged aspect of the construction.

As the building has but one story, and no window is necessary above the porch, the raised lattice in the gable is purely decorative. It is built on a heavy crosspiece and six uprights and suggests the exposed timber construction found in the roof, the window-casings and the porch. This gives the decoration the added charm of consistency. Furthermore, the lattice completes a pleasing proportion of spaces on the front of the house. In merely a passing glance the eye is conscious of the harmony between the narrow cobblestone parapet, the broad shadow of the porch opening, the rough space of clapboarding and the darker area of the lattice. A similar proportion is found in the intervals between the exposed roof supports.

The sharp corners of the porch opening are blunted by two beams running diagonally from the box pillars that support the porch roof to the porch ceiling, and the general outline is softened by a rich curtain of vines. The porch is under the main roof so that the pillars covered with the same siding have the novel appearance of being a continuation of the front wall of the house. It has a concrete floor and is ceiled with narrow pine boards left in the natural color and varnished. The entire building is stained a moss green.

Within, the house is quite as attractive as without. The living room, dining room and the den, connected with the latter by sliding doors, are floored with selected Oregon pine stained to give the effect of Flemish oak. The ceilings are finished with plaster between the box beams, which are set four feet apart.

The fireplace in the living room is very simple; the hearth is of square tiles; the chimneypiece of red brick with a shelf of

C. W. Buchanan, Architect

A CLAPBOARD BUNGALOW OF UNUSUALLY INTERESTING TIMBER CONSTRUCTION, THE HOME OF MR. FURROWS OF PASADENA.

PORCH OF THE BUNGALOW, SHOWING BOX PILLARS AND COBBLESTONE PARAPET.

SHOWING INTERESTING EFFECT OF DINING ROOM RAISED
SEVERAL FEET ABOVE LIVING ROOM FLOOR.

SIMPLE CONSTRUCTION OF FIREPLACE AT ONE END OF THE
LIVING ROOM.

thick pine board. The little casements on either side of the chimneypiece with built-in seats below add a great deal to the interest of that end of the room.

The dining room has the novelty of being raised a step or two above the living room. As is usual in such an arrangement, the length of the two rooms is emphasized. It is the more attractive in this case because the porch, a good-sized room in itself, opens directly into the living room. Thus a very pretty vista is got from either end. The dining room is made especially effective by the amount of woodwork in it, which gives it a character of its own and makes the necessary contrast to the room above which it is raised. It is wainscoted with V-jointed boards to the ceiling, which is rough plastered and tinted a golden brown. Except for the wainscoting in the dining room, the interior walls are all plastered and tinted. The sideboard, about ten feet in width, is built in and runs from floor to ceiling; the doors are of leaded glass. The glint of glass, as one looks into the room, is pleas-

antly repeated by the doors of the book-cases, also built in and running between the square pillars on either side of the steps and the narrow partitions between the living room and dining room.

The arrangement of the rest of the house is given in plan and shows its delightful roominess and ample allowance for closets of every description. The kitchen and bathroom are finished with white enamel.

In view of the beauty and comfort of this little house, the tabulation of cost given below amounts to a surprisingly small total:

Lumber	$700.00
Carpenter Labor	660.00
Mill Work	350.00
Paint and Stain	250.00
Masonry and Plaster	422.00
Hardware	110.00
Electric Work	45.00
Tin and Galvanized Iron	50.00
Plumbing	330.00
Total	$2917.00

SPLIT FIELD STONE AS A VALUABLE AID IN THE BUILDING OF ATTRACTIVE BUNGALOWS AND SMALL HOUSES: BY CHARLES ALMA BYERS

IN this group of six small houses the use of split field stone is especially worthy of notice. The splitting of natural stone brings into sight interesting markings and variegated colors in the rock which are not seen upon the faces that have been exposed to the action of the soil and the weather. This variety in the new surfaces, exposed by the splitting of the stone, makes them blend with almost any color in woodwork and gives a desirable ruggedness to the appearance of a house.

The use of split stones thus treated has been a fairly common custom in the chimneys and foundations of large houses, but there has been a very general feeling that such a heavy material would be quite out of place in a cottage or a bungalow. However, the increase in one-story houses called for an increasing supply and variation in the building materials. Cobblestones were effectively used and these paved the way for an attempt to utilize field stone. Naturally enough, this simple and informal style of architecture found an invaluable aid in the simply prepared masonry, which can be as effectively used inside as outside of the house. A chimneypiece of rough hewn stone fits with delightful appropriateness into a long, low living room, especially where the beams of the ceiling or other structural features are left exposed, and, as the illustrations show, the entire parapets of porches may be made of stone without seeming too heavy for the rest of the house.

The stone may be variously laid; sometimes the joints are trimmed although the faces are left rough, and it may also be laid with the joints following the natural formation of the pieces. In either case, since the faces are comparatively flat, the structural lines are left unbroken, which is not so in cases where the round heads of cobblestones are used. In the houses shown, we find two sorts of stone,—white limestone and two varieties of sandstone,

one red and rather soft and the other a much harder variety of a deep cream color.

In the first house red sandstone is used, finished with trimmed joints. The heavy timbers are of Oregon pine and the siding of the house is cedar shingles. The woodwork is stained to a dark green, in the trimmings and in the supporting construction, which is exposed, it is so deep as to be almost black. The steps and the path are of red cement to match the stonework and the whole makes a rich and artistic color combination. The foundation is also of sandstone, but if this were seen, the house, which is naturally low, would lose too much in height; to obviate this a paneled wainscoting extends around the body of the house and covers all except a narrow strip of the foundation near the ground. The house was built for $3,200.

The second house uses the cream colored sandstone, the frames of the windows painted white to match. The joints of the stone are trimmed and the steps and walk are of cement colored to match. The timbers are rough and square sawn and the house is covered with weatherboarding of Oregon pine, stained to a deep brown. The house is a very low rambling structure containing six rooms, with a large porch, almost a room in itself. The cost of this house was $3,000.

The third house contains eight rooms and the cost is consequently somewhat greater. It was built for about $3,800. The stonework is of white limestone, finished with copings of cement. The pieces are irregular in contour but are carefully selected as to size and shape. The supports of the porch roof as well as the parapets are of the stone, and a stone pergola over the drive at the side of the house will make a most attractive entrance and frame to the garden in the rear when the vines which are planted about it grow up and cover it. The entire house, roof and walls are stained to an emerald green. The

A SMALL CALIFORNIA BUNGALOW COSTING $3,200,
SHOWING THE USE OF RED SANDSTONE FOR PORCH
PILLARS, PORCH FOUNDATION AND CHIMNEY.

A CLAPBOARD HOUSE WITH PORCH FOUNDATION
AND CHIMNEY OF CREAM SANDSTONE AND TRIM-
MING OF CREAM WHITE: COST $3,000.

BUNGALOW COSTING $3,800, WITH WHITE LIME-
STONE USED FOR FOUNDATION, PORCH AND PER-
GOLA: JAPANESE EFFECT IN WOODWORK.

BUNGALOW BUILT FOR $3,300: INTERESTING SIMPLE WOOD CONSTRUCTION, WITH FOUNDATION, PORCH AND PORCH PARAPET OF WHITE LIMESTONE.

$3,000 HOUSE OF WOOD AND STONE, SHOWING COLOR SCHEME OF BLUE-BLACK WOODWORK, WITH WHITE IN STONEWORK AND TRIMMING.

$2,800 CALIFORNIA COTTAGE WITH UNUSUAL WINDOW ARRANGEMENT IN THE ROOF AND WITH PICTURESQUE PORCH PILLARS AND CHIMNEY OF LIMESTONE.

trimmings about the windows are painted white to match the stonework.

In the fourth house the arrangement of the masonry suggests that of the first. This is, however, of white limestone and the joints are not trimmed. Here again we find shingled walls with the wooden paneling covering the foundations. The posts of the porch are very interesting,—a group of four square sawed beams of Oregon pine stand upon the cement coping that finishes the stone posts of the porch. All the woodwork in the house is stained a dark green, except the sashes of the windows, which are white. This house contains seven rooms and the building cost was $3,300.

The fifth house shows more masonry in its construction. Here a pergola continues the porch and extends over the side entrance, and high stone posts rise above the parapet to the eaves of the porch. The color scheme of this house is very peculiar, but nevertheless very attractive. The woodwork is of blue-black stain, and the trimmings are white, as is the limestone used in the masonry. This house was built for $3,000.

The last house of the group, although the smallest and least expensive, since it cost only $2,800, is one of the most interesting structurally. For so small a house it has a great many interesting variations, and yet does not appear crowded or overdecorated. The slant of the roof is very slight, but the house is saved from any appearance of flatness by the shallow dormer which is broken through at the center of the roof, through which light is let in at the top of the living room. Everywhere the timbers used in the construction are left exposed. The porch on the front of the house is largely protected by the main roof and at the side is covered by a pergola construction. The stonework is of white limestone, and the house is stained in two shades of dark green.

In each of the above cases, whatever the color of the house, the stone blends with the surrounding woodwork and adds a certain distinction and solidarity to the whole. With its aid the cottages seem to accomplish that happy position of being neither too dignified nor too insignificant and informal, a position at which it is hard for a small one-story house, not actually in the woods or mountains, to arrive. In most cases the masonry is repeated in the chimneypieces within, and the interior of these houses maintains the same dignified informality which characterizes them from without. Another point in favor of the use of split field stone of any variety is that usually it is so inexpensive. If it had to be quarried and transported to the builder the expense would be a different matter, but in rocky portions of the country when property is being cleared for building, oftentimes a man may find close at hand all the stone that he wants for the small trouble of splitting it.

Another advantage of using the stone native to the environment in the construction of a house is a certain appearance that the house gains of long familiarity with the setting, especially where much of the surrounding property is still left in its natural rugged condition. The use of the stone in the house establishes a link between the building and the country in which it is located that is not the less a powerful influence because it is not obvious. It is these subtle influences that bind a house with neighboring houses or with the landscape, into a pleasing unity that makes us find in some buildings an amount of charm entirely disproportionate to the actual beauty of design that they possess.

Of course, a house must have good structural lines, but it is the attention to matters like these, the taking time to decide correctly whether one style or another of architecture is best suited to the character of the landscape that adds much or takes much from what a house already possesses of beauty and charm.

SUMMER BUNGALOWS IN DELAWARE, DESIGNED TO AFFORD COMFORT IN LITTLE SPACE

THE originals of the five little bungalows illustrated in this article are standing in one of the most attractive portions of the State of Delaware. With the exception of the two larger cottages they are for week-end use and were designed by the owners themselves. The first is of rough pine boards stained brown with white trim. The obvious simplicity of the body of the house is relieved by the rustic porch supports and the curving lines in the railing of twisted withes. The second is built on sloping ground against a charming background of leafy trees and thick underbrush. The body of it is plaster of a gray color; the chimney, which suggests a cozy fireplace within, is built of field stone. The top of the chimney shows an interesting variation in chimney building; it is of plaster held together on the outside with sticks, after the fashion of a crow's nest. The roof and porch hood have not been painted but left to take the stain of the wind and weather, so that in the winter the house is as little noticeable against the bare gray trees as when it is half hidden with summer greenery. There is something delightfully suggestive in the furnishings of the porch; a table, a chair and a book rest. The table is a mere board, the chair is a most primitive support roughly made of boards and unfinished logs, but the book rest has a graceful series of Gothic arches carved upon its supports.

The third bungalow is covered with broad weather-boarding, the porch closed in by rustic trellis-like sides for vines, the roof is of tarred paper, the chimney inside and out of field stone roughly trimmed. Here in a more practical way we get the sense of completeness and comfort, of "much in little"; the little house with its owner pleasantly entertaining a friend on the porch, the vegetable garden in fine and flourishing condition, the pleasant suggestions of shadowy wooded walks to be had for the seeking, and in all probabilities a delightful neighbor near by.

The little cottage called "The Poplars" is perhaps the most picturesque and delightful of all. With the exception of the black tarred-paper roof, it is a soft, weather-stained gray. Meadow grass and the wild flowers brush up against its walls and the poplar trees lean over it from above. Soon the young sapling before the porch will grow up and its branches droop around the entrance, so that the house will hardly be seen for the mass of green about it.

The last bungalow is set in the very midst of the woods. It is less roughly constructed than the others. The beams are trimmed smooth and stained, and the broad porch is screened in so that the living space is practically divided into rooms and porch.

To the people who really love the life of the country and the woods, "to rough it," these little bungalows will unfold the many pleasures that they afford their owners. It is not necessary to have a large house and an elaborate menage to enjoy the country, indeed they are a drawback, a barrier of artificiality, a limitation upon freedom of thought and action. In the city our house is our refuge from noise and turmoil, our library a place for rest and quiet thought. In the country, the woods themselves are the securest cloisters, their clean, sweet aisles insuring perfect peace. The house is but a shelter from the storms, the store house against our material needs, the place where we sleep, although for that, most of us can say truthfully with the simple-hearted philosopher of Syria sleeping under the stars, "The pillow I like best is my right arm."

There can be no doubt in the minds of those who have followed the rather slow development of an architecture adapted to American country life that the bungalow has furnished a most valuable source of inspiration. It was designed in the first place in Eastern countries for the life of intelligent busy people, whose existence is a practical one and whose aim must of necessity be as simple as is con-

A DELAWARE BUN-
GALOW OF ROUGH
PINE BOARDS
STAINED BROWN
WITH WHITE TRIM:
NOTE THE SIMPLIC-
ITY OF CONSTRUC-
TION RELIEVED BY
RUSTIC PORCH SUP-
PORTS AND THE
RAILING OF TWISTED
WITHES: THE CASE-
MENT WINDOWS
ADD A DECORATIVE
TOUCH TO THE
WALLS OF THE
HOUSE, AND THEY
ARE PLACED HIGH
TO FLOOD THE LIT-
TLE ROOMS WITH
LIGHT: AN EXCEL-
LENT MODEL FOR
LOGS OR CEMENT
CONSTRUCTION.

SIDE VIEW OF THE
ABOVE BUNGALOW,
SHOWING THE USE
OF PORCH AS AN
OUTDOOR LIVING
ROOM AS WELL AS
AN ADDED PICTUR-
ESQUE QUALITY AS
TO THE GENERAL
APPEARANCE: THE
ROOF OF TARRED
PAPER IS AN IM-
PORTANT SUGGES-
TION FOR AN INEX-
PENSIVE BUNGA-
LOW: THE SIMPLIC-
ITY OF THE STYLE
OF ARCHITECTURE
WOULD HARMONIZE
CHARMINGLY WITH
ANY PRIMITIVE
SURROUNDINGS.

BUNGALOW OF GRAY
PLASTER WITH
SHINGLED ROOF AND
RUSTIC PORCH SUP-
PORTS: THE ROOF
AND PORCH HOOD
ARE NOT PAINTED,
BUT LEFT TO
WEATHER: THE
CHIMNEY OF FIELD
STONE IS A PICTUR-
ESQUE ADDITION TO
THE TINY COTTAGE:
FOR SO SMALL A
HOUSE THE WIN-
DOWS ARE EXCEP-
TIONALLY WELL
PLACED: THE
SLIGHT EXPENSE OF
BUILDING WOULD
MAKE THIS COT-
TAGE PRACTICABLE
FOR A COUNTRY
PLACE FOR WEEK-
ENDS ONLY.

THIS BUNGALOW IS COVERED WITH BROAD WEATHER-BOARDING: THE PORCH IS CLOSED IN WITH RUSTIC TRELLIS SIDES FOR VINES: THE CHIMNEY IS OF FIELD STONE ROUGHLY TRIMMED, AND TAR PAPER COVERS THE ROOF FOR WARMTH AND SECURITY FROM RAIN: A HOMELIKE NOTE IS GIVEN IN THE FLOURISHING VEGETABLE GARDEN AT ONE SIDE OF THE HOUSE AND THE NEAT LITTLE PATH DIVIDED IT FROM THE FLOWERS.

THIS COTTAGE IS CALLED "THE POPLARS" AND IS PICTURESQUELY SITUATED: MEADOW GRASS AND WILD FLOWERS BRUSH UP AGAINST THE WALLS AND THE POPLAR TREES LEAN OVER AND SHELTER IT FROM ABOVE: WITH THE EXCEPTION OF THE BLACK TAR-PAPER ROOF, THE LITTLE HOUSE IS A SOFT WEATHER-STAINED GRAY, WITH WHITE CASEMENT TRIMMINGS: AN ENCHANTING SPOT FOR WEEK-END VISITS.

CUDDLED BACK IN THE VERY HEART OF THE WOODS THIS BUNGALOW RESTS: IT IS A LITTLE LESS PRIMITIVE IN CONSTRUCTION THAN THE OTHERS: THE BEAMS ARE TRIMMED SMOOTH AND STAINED AND THE BROAD PORCH IS SCREENED IN SO THAT THE LIVING SPACE IS PRACTICALLY DIVIDED INTO ROOMS AND PORCH: IT SUGGESTS A LONGER RESTING TIME THAN A WEEK-END VISIT.

38

sistent with comfort and attractiveness. And although it has gone through many changes in the readjustment to Western ideas of comfort and beauty, fortunately it has not lost in the transition its original fundamental purposes of furnishing space without elaboration, beauty without extravagance and comfort for the least expenditure of time and money.

Of course, there is a wide range of variation shown in the evolution of the bungalow in this country. In some of the Adirondack camps it has grown into an elaborate structure, with a second story added and many sumptuous details of finish and ornament; while in the Delaware week-end or summertime buildings, illustrated in this article, it has diminished into something scarcely more than a shingled cabin, yet even here holding to the better idea of space and to the suggestion of outdoor living on the wide porches. For every bungalow is designed always with the view of outdoor living or else it is not a self-respecting bungalow.

The country homes in America which are essentially an outgrowth of the bungalow, and yet emphatically adapted to our ideas of home life, have grown almost into a definite type of native architecture, so completely have they responded to the realities of the life of the vast majority of American people and this type of architecture, which we almost think of as new, aims not only to provide space for the unencumbered existence which sensible people have grown to demand, but it is adding to its inherent picturesqueness every sort of sane material comfort. And in addition it is also bravely facing the servant problem by seeking to reduce the amount of housework without essentially lessening the actual beauty of the house interior; rather adding to it, in fact, by insisting that, for the first time in the history of our domestic architecture, we shall present right structural line and well thought out color schemes in the interior of our homes, and insisting upon simplicity with beauty.

A MOUNTAIN BUNGALOW WHOSE APPEARANCE OF CRUDE CONSTRUCTION IS THE RESULT OF SKILFUL DESIGN

GREENE and Greene, who are responsible for so much of the interesting domestic architecture of the Pacific coast, are also the architects of this unusual bungalow built in the foothills of the Sierra Madres. These hills form some of the most beautiful scenery of southern California; they are low and sharply defined, swinging up from the rich valleys where the cities and towns are built; their heights are perpetually wound about with scarfs of rose and purple mist, below which emerge the forests of cypress, cedar and redwood, stretching a mantle of ruddy brown foliage down to the very edges of the peaceful olive orchards that cover the low slopes of the hills with their shimmering gray-green crowns. The coloring is intense but not brilliant; the landscape is deep and restful, rugged with frequent masses of richly-toned stone.

The architects, as nearly as it is possible, have reflected the general character of the landscape in the bungalow that they have designed. It is, as the picture shows, low and rambling, the roof low-pitched, with broadly projecting eaves. The foundations and chimneys are of the rough stone; the timbers are all of Oregon pine left rough and undressed, and wherever it is possible in the construction they are left exposed. The siding is of broad boards set upright with the cracks battened down with two-inch straps. The color blends with the ruddy brown of the hills, and the stonework is repeated by the big boulders that are scattered here and there over the property.

One of the chief charms of the house is its roughness; it gives the impression of being a haphazard construction carelessly built to serve as a mountain shelter for vagrant travelers. The native stone that is used in the construction is left quite rough and its arrangement appears to be governed by chance. The chimney, for example, shown in the second illustration, seems hardly more than a great heap of rock, so gradually does it narrow above the unusually broad base. The broad gaps between the stones at the bottom are filled in with the tendrils of an ivy vine which is planted at its base, and in the autumn the red of the foliage, massed irregularly against the gray-brown rock and the deeper toned house form a startlingly beautiful bit of natural decoration.

The bungalow is designed so that it makes a shallow patio or court surrounded on three sides. This space, shaded by the house, is converted into a miniature flower garden, where rustic seats are placed and hammocks swing. The bungalow contains six rooms, two sleeping rooms, besides a living room, den, dining room and kitchen, and all save the kitchen open upon the patio by wide doors set with glass panes above a short panel of wood.

The interior of the house has the same rough character as the exterior. The walls, and the ceiling, following the shape of the roof, are of the same broad boards of Oregon pine, battened at their junctures, but they are more smoothly finished than upon the outside of the house, as also are the timbers and the tie beams. The whole is given the dark stain of weathered oak.

All the furniture possible, such as bookcases, seats, writing desks, the sideboard and so forth, are built into the house, and the use of the broad boards and battens is most effective in the cabinet work. The rest of the furniture has been made especially to match the woodwork. The pieces are heavy and designed after a most simple and primitive model. The rails and posts of the chairs and settles are straight pieces of board, the posts four by four, and the rails nearly two inches thick. All the rails are notched into their supports, the ends projecting beyond and held in place by wooden pins. This rough construction gives an appearance of great strength and ruggedness which is in keeping with the massive fireplaces that heat the living room and den. These fireplaces are built of field stone, with the same effect of rude construction as the chimney outside; the stones are kept in place by inserting the back parts only into cement, and the effect is of a pile of stones built up about the fire, rather than a carefully constructed chimneypiece. A heavy pine board, five by six inches thick, forms the lintel above the fire opening, which is unusually large and has a capacity for huge logs. Above the lintel another heavy board forms a shelf, the ends extending beyond the massive chimney. On the hearth at either side of the fire opening, two boulders project in a natural way from the rest of the stonework and form two delightful fireside seats.

A house of such unusual design cannot but be interesting in itself, and the fittings which have been chosen for it are entirely in keeping with the exterior. Fabrics of Indian manufacture, with their quaint designs and rich coloring, form the hangings for the rooms, and the house contains many lovely pieces of Indian pottery, and baskets and relics of the earlier Indians.

The American bungalow has, at present, more general interest than any other form of house. Whether its rough and rugged exterior and the primitive features of its construction result from the carefully planned effects of some skilful architect, as in the case of this mountain shelter, or from the crude workmanship of the amateur who, following out the instincts of his forbears, builds his own rambling, one-story shack, the bungalow has more individuality than any other sort of dwelling place.

The reason is, in a way, obvious. It is only slowly that architects are getting away from the idea that life is more than "a round of calls and cues" and understanding that the town home may have just as strong an individuality and freedom in its construction, even if it be of a different sort, as a country house. In the bungalow, which is admittedly the shelter of an informal and untrammelled mode of living, the builders have, so to speak, let themselves go, unleashed their fancy, and, restrained only to meet the actual needs of life, have produced a variety of charming and individual structures, ranging from small, week-end houses to two-story buildings for all year use, under the name of bungalow.

And modern Americans are getting farther away, every day, from the formal, prescribed methods of conducting their households and their lives, and consequently are approaching simplicity and spontaneity even in their town life. The former artificiality of living was reflected in the artificiality and formality of the house, inside and out, and even after it began to disappear in practical living, custom made us retain the spirit of it in our architecture. Following the lead of a few clear-sighted builders who saw this gradual change of conditions, the town houses recently built, although showing a solidity and reserve consistent with their surroundings, yet exhibit more character and interest than ever before. It is not too much to say that this period of architecture has responded generously to the influence of the simple, informal bungalow.

Greene & Greene, Architects.
See page 329.

A BUNGALOW BUILT IN THE FOOTHILLS OF THE SIERRA MADRES: THE FOUNDATION AND CHIMNEY ARE OF FIELD STONE, THE TIMBERS ARE UNDRESSED OREGON PINE.

THE CHIMNEY OF THE BUNGALOW BUILT BY GREENE & GREENE HAS
AN ESPECIALLY PICTURESQUE BEAUTY. IT SEEMS TO SPRING FROM
THE GROUND, YET IS AN INHERENT PART OF THE ARCHITECTURE.

BUNGALOW OWNED BY MR. E. A. WEBBER, OF LOS ANGELES: DESIGNED BY MR. ALFRED HEINEMAN.

AN EXAMPLE OF PROGRESSIVE ARCHITECTURE FROM THE PACIFIC COAST: BY HELEN LUKENS GAUT

SO many beautiful and unusual designs for houses come to us from the Pacific Coast, that it would almost seem as if the West were the only home of the new American architecture. It is perhaps natural that this should be so, for the true Westerner is a practical soul, and ever open to suggestions from any quarter which promise to increase his comfort and gratify his sense of beauty. Furthermore, the Californian has the courage of his convictions in building the kind of house that seems to him most suitable for the climate and surroundings of that part of the country. Therefore, he either builds it of concrete, in which case it takes naturally a form resembling that of the old missions; or he builds it of wood, and here we get the influence of the Orient, especially of Japan. This does not mean that both types of houses are not entirely modern and distinctively American, only that the same conditions which created the older forms of building have been met with equal directness in the new.

Therefore the bungalow shown here reminds one distinctly of the Japanese grouping of irregular roof lines, and also of the Japanese use of timbers. Yet there is hardly a feature which one could point out as being derived from the Japanese. The resemblance comes rather from the same appreciation of the decorative possibilities of wood as a building material, and of the modifications that present themselves naturally when the wood is combined with the rough cement blocks and pillars of a part of the construction. Both the shingles and the heavy timbers are of redwood, the rich red brown tone of the oiled wood contrasting pleasantly with the deep biscuit color of the concrete. The decorative use of wood is shown in marked degree in the fence which extends from the back of the house to the stable. The device of wide boards of alternate length, set close together and capped with a heavy square rail, is so simple that the individual effect of such a fence is amazing, and sets us to wondering why most of these high screening fences are so irredeemably ugly when it is such an easy matter to make them beautiful.

This bungalow, which was designed by Mr. Alfred Heineman, a Los Angeles architect, and is owned by Mr. E. A. Webber, of Los Angeles, shows the result of close sympathy and clear understanding between the architect and the owner. It contains eight rooms, with a bathroom, screen porch, large upper screen bedroom, front veranda, patio, cellar and furnace room, and being on one floor it naturally spreads over a fair amount of ground. It is not at all the sort of a building to be put up on a narrow city lot, for in addition to covering a reasonable area of ground itself, it absolutely demands to be set in an ample space of grass and shrubbery, or much of its charm would be hidden.

One of the most charming features of the house is that which marks it as belonging to a warm, sunshiny climate,—the patio on the south side. This is put to precisely the same use as it was in the old Spanish days; that is, much of the family life is carried on out there, the place being made charming

PROGRESSIVE ARCHITECTURE IN THE WEST

with rough, comfortable furniture that can stand exposure to the weather, and with pots and hanging baskets of palms, ferns and flowering plants. A small open space between the pavement and wall of the house allows for a flower bed, so that all the plants are growing and healthy. At night the place is lighted with lanterns of hammered glass that hang in wrought-iron frames from the cross-beams of the pergola. The vines, which will ultimately clamber all over this pergola, have been planted so recently that they have barely reached to the top of the pillars, but when they attain their growth, as they will do within a marvelously short time, the last touch of beauty will have been added to this pleasant outdoor retreat. The admirable arrangement of the bungalow is clearly shown by the floor plan, but a more

PATIO IN MR. WEBBER'S BUNGALOW.

low, there is nothing crude about its finish or construction, either inside or out. The woodwork of the interior is all of redwood, finished so that the satiny surface and beautiful color effects are given their full value. The beams which span the ceilings of the living room, dining room and den are all boxed, as are the massive square posts that appear in the openings between the living room and den and also between the dining room and breakfast room.

A particularly charming effect is given by the arrangement of the tiled chimneypiece in the living room. This is low, broad and generous looking, and the bookcases on either side, with the leaded glass windows above, form a part of the structure which is treated as a whole and fills the entire end of the room. Leaded glass, in beautiful landscape designs and harmonious coloring, is used with admirable effect in the windows above the piano and fireplace, and also in the glass doors of the buffet and book-

LIVING ROOM, LOOKING INTO DEN.

vivid idea of the rooms and their relation to one another may be seen in the reproductions from photographs of the interior. Although this house is distinctly a bunga-

LIVING ROOM, SHOWING FIREPLACE.

cases. The den, which forms a part of the living room, is treated in much the same way as the larger room, save that its walls are wholly paneled with wood, and in a recess at one side of the window is built a wall bed which can be let down when necessary, converting the room into an additional bedroom to be used when the house is full. The opening into the dining room is so wide that it also seems to be a part of the living room. The ceiling differs from that of the other room in that it runs up to a slight peak where a massive girder affords support for the cross-beams. The walls of this room are paneled with redwood to the height of the plate rail, and the wall space above is covered with tapestry paper in a low-toned forest design. The large buffet is built in, and with the china closet above, extends to the ceiling.

Just off the dining room is a small breakfast room which, with its wide bay window, is hardly more than a very large window nook that is flooded with sunshine in the morning, and is a delightful place for breakfast. It is also used as a supplementary dining room when enter-

tainments are given.

The same taste that ruled the building and decorating of this house also directed its furnishing, so that the furniture falls readily into place as a part of the whole scheme of things, and harmonizes completely with the woodwork and the whole style of construction. It is not often that one sees this because, although people may build an entirely new house, they usually go into it laden with possessions which are dear to them, but which can hardly be said to harmonize with the structural scheme of a modern bungalow. In this case, however, the furniture might have been chosen with a special reference to this house. Even the Turkish rugs, ordinarily so difficult to reconcile with the slightly rugged effect that usually prevails in a bungalow, are quite at home here, because the whole interior finish is so com-

DINING ROOM, SHOWING BUILT-IN SIDEBOARD.

plete and delicate that the house affords an admirable setting for Oriental rugs.

Plenty of outdoor sleeping accommodations are afforded because a screen porch opens from one of the bedrooms, and upstairs is a large screen room which gives ample accommodation to all who care to sleep out-of-doors. This upstairs screen room is not only a convenience, but its presence adds much to the exterior beauty of the house, as it gives an opportunity for a slight

into a sunroom by the addition of a glass roof and a front wall of glass in place of the pergola and pillars. With a southern exposure this would mean a delightful sunroom and conservatory, especially in winter,

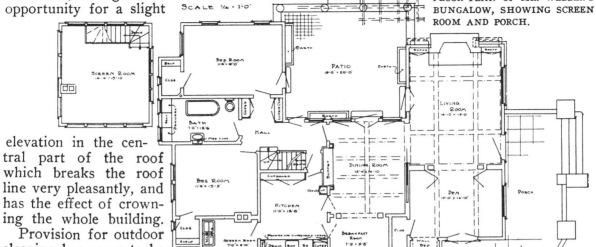

FLOOR PLAN OF MR. WEBBER'S BUNGALOW, SHOWING SCREEN ROOM AND PORCH.

elevation in the central part of the roof which breaks the roof line very pleasantly, and has the effect of crowning the whole building.

Provision for outdoor sleeping has come to be as much a matter of course in the East as it is in the West, and this screen room would be particularly well adapted to the Eastern climate, because the widely overhanging roof affords plenty of shelter even from driving storms. Also in an Eastern climate it might be advisable to transform the patio

as it would get all the sunshine there is and would also be sheltered from cold and wind by the walls of the house. If the glass roof gave too much light the open space could, of course, be roofed over in the ordinary way.

A CALIFORNIA BUNGALOW, DESIGNED BY
MR. CHAS. E. SHATTUCK, OF LOS ANGELES.

A CHARMING AND INEXPENSIVE COTTAGE IN THE BUNGALOW STYLE: BY HELEN LUKENS GAUT

HERE is yet another bungalow from the land of bungalows,—southern California. It was designed by Mr. Charles E. Shattuck, a Los Angeles architect, and was built in that city. It is a plan that may easily be adapted to the requirements of an Eastern climate, especially as it is carefully finished in every detail, being meant for a permanent dwelling instead of a summer camp or vacation home. Like most California houses it is built of wood, and the red brick used for the chimney and the pillars of the pergola blends well with the warm brown tones of the timbers and shingles.

The plan is admirable in the regard for convenience and comfort shown in the arrangement of the rooms, and in the economy of space that gives a larger amount of room than would seem possible within the limits of a small house. The house itself seems really larger than it is, because, being all on one floor, it is long and wide in proportion to its height, and the low-pitched, wide-eaved roof has a splendid straight sweep giving the effect as well as the actuality of shelter.

By a rather unusual arrangement, the big outside chimney is at the front of the house, and the entrance from the street to the recessed porch, which runs partly down the side, is at the corner. Beyond this there is a good-sized porte-cochère, sheltered by a pergola supported upon massive square brick pillars that taper slightly toward the top. Both roof and walls of the bungalow are covered with shingles, left unpainted so that they may take on the delightful tones of silvery gray and brown that only the

LOOKING THROUGH THE PERGOLA PORTE COCHERE.

weather can give. The foundation is entirely hidden by shrubs and flowers that grow close to the walls, and the woodbine that partially covers the chimney softens the severity of its straight lines. Between the pillars of the porte-cochère are heavy iron chains, which have been allowed to rust to a rich golden brown color, and be-

COTTAGE IN BUNGALOW STYLE

LIVING ROOM, SHOWING INGLENOOK.

hind them a high lattice clothed with vines shelters the house from its next-door neighbor. The window frames are painted white, so that they form high lights in the general color scheme and repeat the white of the cement walk, steps and floor of the recessed porch.

The interior of the bungalow is plastered throughout, and all the walls and ceilings are tinted in harmonizing tones of cream, brown and old gold. The woodwork, of which there is a great deal, is all brown, and the floors are of oak. The massive mantel of red-brown brick seems to center in itself the warmth of the whole color scheme. On the side of the living room opposite the fireplace is a deep alcove which was built and used by the original owner for installing a pipe organ,

but is now used for a cushioned recess. Bookcases with wooden doors extend across the entire end of the room, and a line of latticed windows fills the space between these cabinets and the plate rail that runs just below the plaster frieze. More bookcases with leaded glass doors extend up the side of the room to the corner of the recess. On either side of the fireplace are two large windows, so that the room is amply lighted.

A small hall with a built-in seat connects the living room with the dining room, and also with the rear hall which affords a means of communication to

DINING ROOM.

the bedrooms and the bath. The treatment of the dining room differs only in minor details from that of the living room. A high wainscot has panels of dark brown leather paper, divided with four-inch stiles set eighteen inches apart. This wainscot is topped with a wide plate rail, and the wall above is tinted to a soft tone of light buff. The ceiling, like that of the living room, is spanned with beams, and the plaster panels between are tinted to the same color as the walls. All the furniture in the dining room is of cedar, and was specially designed by

LIVING ROOM, WITH GLIMPSE OF DINING ROOM.

COTTAGE IN BUNGALOW STYLE

the owner to express his own ideas.

The two bedrooms, with the bathroom between and the screened sleeping porch, are at the rear of the house. A small room for the servant opens off the kitchen, which is equipped with all modern conveniences. As the bungalow was built, it would be suitable for any climate, as it has hot and cold water, electric lights, a good cellar, furnace and all the other comforts that are required in the East, but are more or less optional in the mild California climate. The approximate cost in Los Angeles, where the house was built, was, including fences, woodshed and cement walks, $3,500. It would probably cost more to build a bungalow of this size and design in any part of the East, as

DETAIL OF PERGOLA CONSTRUCTION.

the vicinity of Los Angeles than it is in the neighborhood of New York or Boston, for example. Of course, much would depend upon the attitude of the owner toward the work, as this materially affects the cost of building a dwelling. If he gave the matter his personal attention, hired his men in the most economical way, and saw to it that he obtained his building materials at the lowest possible cost, the price of the house would be considerably less than the estimate given by the average contractor. A great deal of difference also arises from the kind of materials used. If an expensive hardwood is chosen for the interior woodwork, the price goes up instantly. Fortunately, beautiful effects can be obtained by the right use of comparatively inexpensive native woods, and if the owner has sufficient skill in the treatment of wood to finish the woodwork of both exterior and interior himself, one considerable item of expense will be lopped off in the beginning. A house finished, like this one, in redwood costs comparatively little in California, where this beautiful wood is abundant, easily obtained and not at all expensive. If the house were built in the East, it might

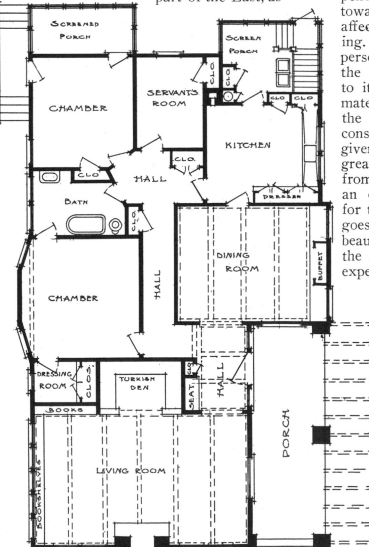

FLOOR PLAN OF BUNGALOW.

the cost of labor and building materials is considerably less in be done in quite as economical a way by the use of some wood native to the locality.

A CALIFORNIA BUNGALOW TREATED IN JAPANESE STYLE: BY ARNOLD L. GESELL

THERE were a few things the builder of this bungalow was sure of from the start: It should be an outdoor house, suited to rural surroundings —light, open, airy, unplastered and unpapered. It should also be a long, low structure like the Mexican hut whose simple, comfortable, horizontal lines seem architecturally so harmonious with the landscape and atmosphere of our Western country.

MINIATURE OF BUNGALOW

MEXICAN HUT WHICH FURNISHED BUNGALOW SUGGESTION.

Another primary suggestion came from the beautiful tall eucalyptus tree (which often grows beside the Mexican hut). This tree is one of the characteristic features of southern California. Though a native of Australia, it thrives on the Pacific Coast almost as though indigenous to the soil, and promises to be one of the great resources of the State; dressed and polished, it rivals mahogany. Its clean pinkish-gray bark also adapts it to unfinished, rustic uses.

To begin with, we made rough sketches of a long, low house, with eucalyptus beams. An arts and crafts friend became interested

BUNGALOW WOODWORK IN JAPANESE STYLE

and suggested a clever way by which the walls of the house could be sturdily constructed of one-inch boards, overlapped in a manner to make unnecessary the use of flimsy battens.

We built a miniature house at the start. It is hard for the untrained mind to think in three dimensions, and the putting together of the house model suggested many possibilities which a struggle with pencil on a plane surface alone could never have done. This miniature took the place of architect's drawings. In fact, we did not use blue prints at all; we planned as we built, rather than the reverse. The fourteen corners of the house were first put up; then the placing of the long, spacious windows was determined, and the walls were literally built around the windows. The partitions were all located for the first time after the floor was down. The fireplace was planned the night before we were ready to use the stone. Much of the furniture was built into the

PYROGRAPHIC OUTFIT FOR TREATING WOOD.

house as we proceeded, and was adapted to its lines and angles. Everybody, even visitors, had a chance to give constructive suggestions. And so the house changed, grew and took shape under our combined hands.

From the road you can hardly see the embowered bungalow; but you catch glimpses of it through the large, leafy English walnut and the dark green orange trees. A prim brick walk leads past a little "public bird bath" and, under the wide-spreading walnut boughs, to the broad front door, or through the long rustic pergola built of unhewn eucalyptus tree trunks. At the further front corner is a eucalyptus stairway which takes you to a roof lookout where you can see stretches of lovely mountains. Not a board in the house was painted, varnished or stained; but every piece was literally charred and brushed on each exposed face and edge before it became a part either of the structure or the furniture. It was a laborious task, but not without recompense, for under this pyrographic treatment even the least interesting wood becomes beautiful, taking on a soft brown corrugated sheen.

Our method was as follows: Each board was placed on a rough easel; the hot blast of a plumber's double-mouthed torch was applied until the whole surface was distinctly charred. Merely scorching the wood to a cloudy brown is an easy matter; it is the charring to a crisp black which take patience—and brings the reward. The intense heat fashions the character of the wood; it burns the hard fiber a permanent strong dark brown and the soft fiber it

SHOWING METHOD OF CONSTRUCTION.

BUNGALOW WOODWORK IN JAPANESE STYLE

THE SECLUDED COURTYARD.

the wall boards and the ribbons are filled with "filler blocks" (shown dark in the picture). The whole is tightly bound together by 4-inch carriage bolts, inserted through the middle axis of each board to allow for shrinkage and expansion, without splitting.

This triple-bound, triple-bolted wall, with a gross diameter of 4 inches, makes a staunch support for the heavy eucalyptus beams, and has an individual beauty besides. The top and bottom ribbons, with their regularly recurring bolt heads, make a pleasing border for the interior of each room and for the exterior of the house. The upright boards alternate in such a manner that every wall, inside and out, forms a series of raised and sunken panels.

The back doorway is nothing more than a comfortable arch between a large orange and a large lemon tree. These two trees complete the enclosure of a secluded quadrangular court which is really a central room. The floor of this court is a soft red brick pavement; the roof is the azure California sky.

From the court you can peep into the kitchen. Sink, cooler, closet, bins are all within arm's reach, compactly contrived to save steps. And every piece of wood is

completely incinerates. When a board has been charred it looks no more promising than a slab which might have come from the ruins of a burned building; but under the plowing, biting attack of the stiff steel butcher's brush what transformation! A dozen hard strokes, and nature's hidden pattern emerges into beautiful relief. If you discount the hard work this brushing is most fascinating and interesting; the burning is especially so done in the quiet dark of the night.

After the boards were burned, brushed and sawed, the walls were reared, but without nails. First, the fourteen corners, each consisting of two upright boards at right angles; then long ribbons (6 inches wide) were strung horizontally from corner to corner. There are three pairs of these ribbons, one at the top, forming the roof plate, one in the middle and one at the bottom. The method of construction is shown in the illustration. (A door, built like the walls, has been taken from its hinges and laid on its side to show a sectional view.) The ribbons serve as binders for the wall boards (12 inches wide), which are placed upright with an overlap of 1½ inches. The alternate open spaces (9 inches wide) between

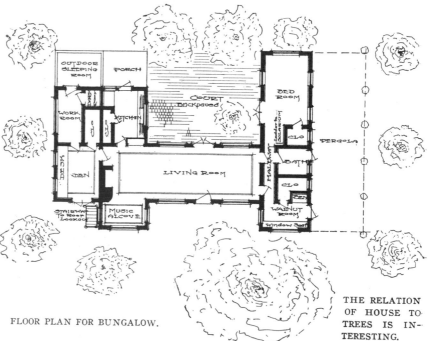

FLOOR PLAN FOR BUNGALOW.

THE RELATION OF HOUSE TO TREES IS INTERESTING.

BUNGALOW WOODWORK IN JAPANESE STYLE

pyrographed and brushed, so that in finish the kitchen is as attractive as any part of the house. Why shouldn't it be?

In the outdoor sleeping room the woodwork is not so impressive, for the walls are almost all screens—with a mesh wide enough to admit sweet air from orchard and mountains.

Adjoining the outdoor sleeping room is a workshop, with carpenter's bench and tools. Brushing aside a curtain made of the long pendant strings of eucalyptus acorns you enter the den. This looks like a workshop, too, with its long, wide desk built like a shelf along one whole side of the wall. The wood in the den has a darker tone, because though pyrographed in the same manner as the other wood, it was brushed *with* the grain instead of *crosswise*. Orange trees shade the windows on one side; on the other is the soft brown masonry of the fireplace, and a little stone wall. Through the lattice above the wall you may peep into the living room.

Returning to the court you pass through French doors into the bedroom. This room has a special charm. An orange tree, with its deep green leaves and golden fruit, presses close against the many-paned window at the end, giving an effect in color and design more wonderful than anything possible in stained-glass art. The room is built

FIREPLACE IN LIVING ROOM.

of California redwood, soft in texture and delicate in its pervading salmon hue. Gold-colored curtains add a little extra glory to the sunlight.

A hallway leads to a cozy room with a long seat and a generous window through which an English walnut tree almost forces its way. A wallbed is built into the closet of this room. By a peg ladder, constructed after the primitive log-cabin style, you can climb onto the sundeck. This deck is really nothing more than the "floored ceiling" of the closets and bath below. A big skylight overhead makes of it a solarium, which gathers precious sunshine in the cool weather.

From the sundeck one can peer down and through the eucalyptus beams and rafters into the long living room. This extensive room is the delight of the bungalow. It is literally bathed in sunlight. Through the sundeck windows at one end, through the chimney transom and skylight at the other, through the variegated panes of art glass in the eaves and through the long windows on either side, the sun comes in. In the cool but sunny weather which prevails through most of the California year, this big airy room is kept at a delightful natural warmth. When the weather is warmer a space two feet wide, extending the

CORNER OF LIVING ROOM.

BUNGALOW WOODWORK IN JAPANESE STYLE

whole length of the ridgepole, can be opened.

The ridgepole was a tall, straight eucalyptus tree, which it took two strong horses to drag. Unhewn and unspliced, it extends from the sundeck into the masonry of the fireplace, a distance of 36 feet. The rafters, crossbeams and ridgepole are all held together, like Solomon's temple, by stout wooden pegs. On one of the crossbeams sits an Arctic owl, on another the carved home of two cuckoos from the Black Forest.

The appointments of the living room are most simple. The double crotch of an orange tree with a redwood top serves as a table; the bookshelves with long curving sides are built in at the ends of windows and benches. The absence of excessive furniture is perhaps one reason why so many people can gather and chat with ease in this one room. It is easily converted into a banquet hall by swinging the long table from the crossbeams and drawing up the benches.

comfortable instead of a ponderous and stiff appearance. It makes a pretty stone-wall partition and at the same time an effective mantelpiece for vase, fruit and flowers. Through a grating made of beautiful burnt wood, you get glimpses of the adjoining den and of the green and gold orange groves beyond. It is especially interesting to note the relation of house to trees.

One feels in the description of this house, at once its individuality and its utility. It is especially suited to the needs of the people who planned and built it. It is arranged to satisfy their ideal of beauty and their idea of comfort. It is planned for plenty of air and sunlight, for outdoor life, and for the mental rest which comes from peaceful vistas and well-harmonized color.

All together it is not the kind of house these particular people could ever have bought finished. The ready-to-use house is built to sell, not use; it is an investment, not a dwelling place. You have got to be intimate with the construction of your house,

VIEW OF BUNGALOW HIDDEN IN WALNUT AND ORANGE TREES.

An alcove makes room for a couch and piano. The long window above the piano is far more alluring than a landscape painting, for it frames an ever-changing view of the distant mountain tops. The house holds many vistas, glimpses and cross-glimpses, and the eye wanders on many journeys through the transom windows, French doors and skylights.

The walls, the drapery, the benches, the carpet and the fireplace all are brown or fawn color.

One of the happiest features of the living room is the low lateral extension of the chimney. It gives the whole fireplace a

to have a sense of intimacy in the finished structure. No one can make a home for you, any more than a character can be developed for you, and the more of yourself that goes into the designing and building of the place in which you are going to live the more happiness you'll get out of living there.

This bungalow with Japanese finish is like a family friend to the owners. It expresses old theories, new points of view, hopes for the future and memories of the past, and incidentally is a message to others who wish to build, telling them to follow out the fundamental idea, not the floor plans, for their joy and peace of mind.

BUNGALOW IN PASADENA, CAL., DESIGNED BY EDWARD E. SWEET.

A CALIFORNIA BUNGALOW OF STONE AND SHINGLE WORTH STUDYING, BOTH IN DESIGN AND INTERIOR FINISH

THAT it is wise to put new wine in new bottles cannot be doubted, and that it is the part of wisdom to put new architecture in new lands is also true. The West is not as yet put to the sad necessity of building houses in perpendicular form, "standing room only," on tip-toe to catch a bit of sun and air! They can assume a comfortable horizontal position, lounging at ease in the midst of gardens! The long low-sweeping line of roof of these charming bungalow-houses permits a beauty such as is often obtained in the "sheer" of a boat.

The accompanying photographs of a house built by Edward E. Sweet of Pasadena, California, at a cost of only $3,500.00 is an excellent type of the commodious, beautifully proportioned bungalows now becoming known as Californian —the new architecture of a new land. This building grows from a rock foundation quite as vegetation springs from the earth, the chimneys rising above it as large rocks occasionally lift their gray heads above the grass and flowers associated with them

DINING ROOM IN BUNGALOW.

in the lawns of Nature's making.

The use of shingles forms a distinct decorative note; the beams and cobbles are handled in a most interesting way; the windows are pleasant spots placed happily in the composition, and the roof completes the whole in a satisfactory manner. Nothing jars, but every feature unites in forming a house of exceptional beauty.

The arrangement of the interior is no less satisfying, combining comfort, convenience, privacy, simplicity, yet creating a luxurious sense of space. The large living room with its reading table within comfortable proximity to the fireplace, a smaller room joined in

BUNGALOW LIVING ROOM.

CALIFORNIA BUNGALOW WORTH STUDYING

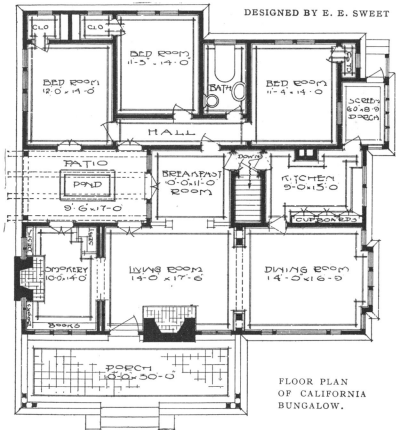

DESIGNED BY E. E. SWEET

FLOOR PLAN OF CALIFORNIA BUNGALOW.

easy access to the patio.

This patio provides another feature of great interest, in its endless possibilities for the enjoyment of outdoor teas, moonlight nights, flowers, vines, fountains, hammocks.

The picturesque use of beams throughout the whole house and the harmonious repetition of the curve of them at the windows appeals to one as a unifying note of exceptional charm. The built-in sideboard and china closets in the dining room show that compactness is a phase of beauty if rightly understood and used. The interior finish of woodwork, the method of lighting, the polished floors add their distinct characteristics to the general effect of substantiality and charm.

The color scheme of the exterior deserves especial consideration, for there are no sudden contrasts of positive color to disturb the eye. The concrete walk joins with the stone foundation, flows into it as one undivided tone. The green of the grass is caught again at the entrance palms and patio vines. The redwood beams and shingles are as one, and the glimpse of chimneys above the roof holds it all together with the foundation, binding the separate parts into a perfect whole.

The type of architecture is eminently suitable to the land, for it is low like the foot-hills about it, broad and substantial.

social manner to the larger room, with no sense of lonesome separateness, yet giving certain seclusion to the smokers or perhaps the young students of the household, suggest hominess, joy of family life.

A large dining room for the formal dinner, a cozy breakfast room just off the patio where glimpse of a pond can be seen, where perhaps a fountain plays or waterlilies grow, provides perfect dining room facilities.

The three bedrooms at the rear give quiet seclusion to sleepers, are within convenient proximity to the bathroom and have

A SECOND VIEW OF $3,500.00 CALIFORNIA BUNGALOW.

A CALIFORNIA BUNGALOW OF ORIGINALITY AND CHARM

A BUNGALOW BUILT IN LOS ANGELES, CAL., BY REGINALD HARRIS.

IT would be difficult for even a stranger, much less an acquaintance, to pass by this house without entering and making himself happily at home upon the cool wide porch! Its invitation is so evident, so genuine and irresistible that it seems to include the world at large as well as intimate friends. The soft green of the rugs and wicker chairs, the palms and ferns so excellently placed, the rich color of the wood, combine to weave a lure that is almost peremptory. The low railing around this porch is an interesting feature, forming a convenient receptacle for a magazine, book, workbasket or pot of flowers, as well as adding a cozy sense to what is essentially an outdoor living room. Everyone likes to sit on the railing around a porch, no matter how high, frail or uncomfortable it is, and this low, broad, substantial balustrade permits such treatment in comfort and safety. Such a simply constructed railing should be a joy to any housekeeper, for it is free from the obstructions found on most porch railings that make it difficult to keep the floor well swept.

The most distinctive feature of this charming Los Angeles bungalow is the roof, which the architect, Reginald Harris, has treated in the bold and original manner so suitable to California architecture. The immense overhang of it, the grace of its sweeping lines, the balance of one line with another, the composition of the whole, the management and arrangement of the upper and lower roof areas are distinctly original and decidedly beautiful and give an air of magnificence to a house that is really very simple and inexpensive. The house is a typical bungalow in the height of its ceilings, which are eight feet six inches downstairs and seven feet six inches upstairs, and the low, gradual, broad sweep of the roof lines keep the two-story house within conventionalized bungalow limits. The large copper lantern is in admirable keeping with the general style of breadth and grace, adding a note of welcome at night, throwing a soft, subdued light over every-

DETAIL OF THE PORCH SHOWING INTERESTING USE OF CONCRETE.

A CALIFORNIA BUNGALOW OF ORIGINALITY AND CHARM

thing. French windows opening from the dining room make it easy to move the table out on the porch, that the breakfast, luncheon or tea may be served there.

The interior of this home is simple, convenient and comfortable. Large windows and doors made of glass let in plenty of light and air and are so arranged that they make a decorative note in the general design of the exterior. The outside of this commodious house is of ordinary weather boarding with concrete pillars and chimney, and ruberoid roof.

The living-room walls and ceilings are finished in Oregon pine stained the soft green that can be so successfully obtained on this wood. In every room is to be found some useful built-in features. In the sitting room are bookcases, in the dining room a buffet, and cabinets in the kitchen, chests of drawers in the bedroom. Economy of space is thus obtained, a convenient place for everything is assured, and a decorative effect in each room is produced which is attractive and satisfying in every particular.

The walls and ceiling of the dining room are also finished in Oregon pine, with the exception of the frieze introduced above the plate rail. This frieze adds to the sense of outdoors given to the room by the large windows and glass doors, for it shows a bit of forest, just such a glimpse of trees and soft skies as would be seen through real windows. The frieze of trees, continuing from window to window, gives an apparent outdoor view without a break around the whole room, so that the dining table seems to be set at the edge of a forest glade, the real open windows giving a vista of sunny plains.

Another interesting feature of this house is the outdoor sleeping room, which is entered from the upper hall, through large French windows. These outdoor bedrooms have come to be as much a part of a Californian house plan as the kitchen, dining room or reception room, for whoever has once slept in the open air never willingly shuts himself up in the ordinary old-time bedroom again. Almost everyone in this favored clime has, through friend or hotel, been given an oppor-

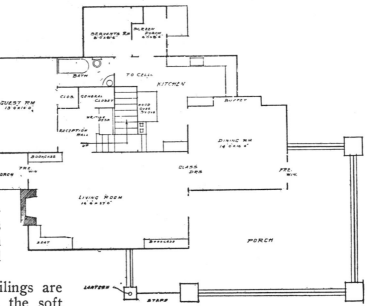

CALIFORNIA BUNGALOW: FIRST FLOOR PLAN.

tunity to sleep in one of these starlit rooms and at once the ambition to possess such a sweet, wholesome bedroom takes possession of the guest or traveler. So hardly a home is to be found without such a bedroom, either built especially for such purpose or else created as successfully as possible from some porch.

In this sleeping room a disappearing bed is installed which permits the room to be used as outdoor sitting or sewing room during the day, the bed itself forming a comfortable seat and convenient lounging place.

The bedrooms are all finished in white, which is a universally satisfactory way of finishing sleeping or dressing rooms because of the resultant lightness, freshness, cleanliness, airiness.

Nothing expensive has been installed in this house. It is just another of the many beautiful bungalows being constructed by home-makers and architects throughout the

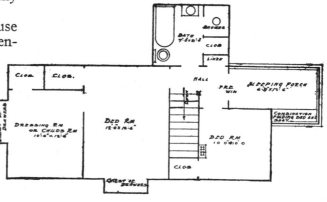

CALIFORNIA BUNGALOW: SECOND FLOOR PLAN.

A CALIFORNIA BUNGALOW OF ORIGINALITY AND CHARM

VIEW OF THE OUTDOOR LIVING ROOM.

West. The immense overhang of the roof creates the shade so much to be desired at midday in this sunny land, besides adding the distinct note of originality and beauty to the building. This bungalow, so simple, informal, comfortable, "homey" in every way, could be duplicated, considering the number of rooms it contains, for a price surprisingly low, because it is so free from unnecessary ornament or display.

The floor plan is well worth a careful study by anyone wishing to build a home where economy of space is to be a feature, for there is no waste of double partitions, no unnecessary hall space. The rooms fit together with the utmost ease, apparently, yet all home-builders know that this is the result of careful planning. All the measurements are broad and generous, like the entrance to the house itself, and also the passages from one room into another. The vistas from room to room, the charming use of glass doors from living room into dining room and the French door from the dining room onto the porch, give a sense of space, as of one great room barely walled from the weather. The many windows and the sun-porch extension heighten this

sense of outdoor life. Certainly as much of the light, cheer and vigor of the out-of-doors is retained as is possible in any house.

The centering of stairways leading up to the bedrooms and down to the basement, with the several closets, is an excellent arrangement of great working convenience and an example of wise use of wall space —which simplifies building. This use of the inner walls for household convenience leaves the outer walls free for an abundance of large windows. Where there is not a window it is because there is a door leading to a porch. The kitchen porch is well placed for entry and usefulness generally.

In the second floor plan can be seen the same simple arrangement of rooms that distinguishes the first floor. The many closets and the built-in chests of drawers lead one to believe that the housekeeper must be a perfectly satisfied one, for certainly the rooms are amply provided with these necessities of order and convenience. The plan shows the sleeping porch with the bed which closes into a lounging couch or seat during the day, thus converting the sleeping porch of the night into an outdoor sitting room for use during the daylight hours.

CORNER OF OUTDOOR LIVING ROOM.

A CALIFORNIA BUNGALOW OF ORIGINALITY AND CHARM

It is hard to find more ideal conditions for the exercising of an architect's ingenuity and good taste than in this western land. The cost of construction is much less than in the East because the necessity of meeting the severity of winter is done away with. The problems of plumbing, lighting and heating are reduced to a minimum, so that an architect can devote the major part of his skill to creating beauty. Elsewhere these three problems sometimes d r i v e beauty of line into the background and they also demand so large a part of the price set aside for the construction of the home that there is little left to be devoted to the beauty without which a home is built in vain.

INDOOR LIVING ROOM LOOKING INTO DINING ROOM

The West, or rather the people who are drawn to seek a home in the West, encourage simplicity of living. And simplicity of living permits simplicity of building. It also encourages originality in every direction, the builder's ideal being not to build as others have built, but to build as he himself desires. And when people dare to be true to themselves there is bound to be a great manifestation of originality. For it is the slavish obedience to custom or precedent that makes for monotony, and monotony leads to degeneration. A copy of a copy is the surest way in the world to lose the beauty that marked the original and that prompted the first copy. Just as no two people are alike in character, but each interesting in some especial direction, so no two homes would be alike, but each interesting and beautiful in a separate way if the builders of the houses would but exercise the individuality they find in themselves. Since the West encourages originality in every way and scoffs at the dulness that knows only how to imitate, the homes of its people, the office buildings, stores, bridges are marked by a freshness of design that furnishes one of the chief charms of the Pacific Coast. Every effort is made to have each new home different from all others, not that it may rival its friend and neighbor, but that the beauty of each and the civic beauty of the whole community may be enhanced. Imitation in architecture is not the "sincerest form of flattery"; it is a form of cheapening.

ONE CORNER OF DINING ROOM.

HOW I BUILT MY BUNGALOW: BY CHARLOTTE DYER

Illustrated by Helen Lukens Gaut.

FRONT VIEW OF CALIFORNIA BUNGALOW, SHOWING COVERED AND PERGOLA PORCH.

LIKE most young girls I built a "castle in the air" and waited for the "fairy prince." My "castle" was a bungalow. I studied descriptions and illustrations of these pretty little houses far more earnestly that I did my Latin or the fashions, and waited. Of course, I knew I should never have a bungalow of my own until after the arrival of the "fairy prince." And at last, however, though even now it seems too good to be true, every wish is realized. My "castle," without a bump, a thump or a bruise, has settled gracefully to terra firma, and my "fairy prince" has come and has turned into a king, and we are, as the story books say, going to live happily ever after.

We started housekeeping in an apartment house, but we both hated such a life. Electric cars whizzed and rumbled in front of us, while a bull terrier and a poll parrot barked and shrieked at the back of us. We wanted to be quiet and alone, and almost at once we began looking for a ready-made bungalow into which we could move our bags and baggage, and in which we could turn our unrest into peace. We looked at scores of houses, and while we didn't feel we were especially hard to please, we couldn't find anything that just suited. We wanted a view of the mountains, and we knew we wouldn't be satisfied with anything else. Several friends said: "Why don't you buy the lot you want and design and build your own house?" I told them I couldn't do such a thing as design a house, that I knew absolutely nothing about building. I kept their suggestion in mind, however, and the more I thought about it, the more I thought that perhaps I could design my house. Whenever I passed a bungalow in course of construction, I looked over the foundation, framework, finish, etc., until I acquired a certain familiarity with house construction.

About this time I met a woman whose business was that of designing and building houses to sell. She was most proficient in her line, in fact, had made a small fortune in this work. She encouraged me to go ahead and build my bungalow, saying she would be glad to help me in any way. These talks with her gave me inspiration and courage, and very soon I began the actual planning and superintendence of our home. I decided not to engage an architect. I knew exactly what I wanted, and so often an architect will insist on incorporating his own ideas, and I wanted just us, my husband and myself, in the "thought" of our home. I wanted a bit of our personality driven in with every nail.

We now began lot hunting in earnest, and finally found one that pleased us im-

HOW I BUILT MY BUNGALOW

SIDE VIEW OF BUNGALOW.

mensely, for it had a long sweeping view of valley and mountains. This lot, however, was somewhat small, only 40 by 120 feet, and we had set our hearts on having one with at least sixty-feet frontage. On making inquiry we found that the adjoining lot was for sale, so we decided to buy both of them. After holding a "family" consultation, we made up our minds to build a long narrow bungalow on a part of one of the lots, leaving the balance to increase the size of the other lot, on which we intended to build later on. As neither of us had ever built before, we concluded

to call this first house our experiment, a sort of elementary schooling to fit us for building the next, which was to be, so we then thought, our real home. We planned to live in the "experiment" for a little while, then sell at an advance, or rent it. But that was at the beginning. Now that the Bungalow is finished and we are living in it, we have neither desire nor intention of giving it up. Scarce a week passes that some real-estate agent does not stop to inquire if the bungalow is for sale, and somehow I can't help feeling a bit indignant that anyone should suggest my giving it up. I watched it grow so lovingly, from the first thought and foundation stone, to the last timber and pot of paint, and I prize every board and shingle and nail in it as if they were piece and parcel of my very soul.

While there is nothing very technical in building a small bungalow, there are lots of little points to be considered, and lots to be avoided. The very first thing to do is to find an honest carpenter foreman, one, if possible, who has some understanding of drawing up plans

FIREPLACE CORNER IN BUNGALOW, SHOWING INTERESTING WALL TREATMENT AND FURNISHINGS.

HOW I BUILT MY BUNGALOW

and specifications. My architect friend sent out the right man to me with highest recommendations, and I immediately engaged him to draw up the plans at my suggestion, and to act as carpenter foreman on the job. Fortunately he was an excellent draughtsman.

During the previous month I had made as thorough a study of bungalow construction as I could. I always carried a rule and spent much time measuring the width of shakes and the number of inches they were laid to the weather, in fact I measured the heights and depths and widths of everything that interested me, and took particular note of building materials of all sorts, so that I was able to explain with a certain degree of accuracy, just what I wanted. I couldn't see any reason why plans and specifications should be drawn up, for I was to have the work done by the day, and intended to give it my personal supervision, but my friend advised me strongly to have them, so there could be no possible chance of confusion or misunderstanding with the workmen. She said I should sublet contracts for the plumbing and the masonry, the electric wiring and the roofing; in this case plans and specifications would be absolutely necessary to

THE LIBRARY END OF THE LIVING ROOM.

bind the contractors. When the plans were all ready, work began in earnest. My husband had urgent business affairs to look after at this time, and seeing how deeply interested I was, and feeling confidence in me, inexperienced though I was, he gave me entire charge of buying the materials and the superintendence of the building. At first I was a bit nervous and several times asked advice of my friend. After the first week, however, I gained independence and relied entirely on my own wits and judgment to carry me through safely. I employed four men, a working foreman at $4.00 a day, a carpenter at $3.50, a helper for $2.50, and a painter at $3.15, and just nine weeks after the first foundation stone was laid, the house was completed.

I felt that a bungalow to be harmonious, must have a low, flat roof, and the only difficulty I had with my foreman was in trying to convince him that a roof with a pitch of one to six would be practicable. But I had my way in this, as in all things, and the roof is quite satisfactory. Instead of shingles I had asbestos roofing, which is white and contrasts attractively with the

GLIMPSE OF DINING ROOM OUT OF LIVING ROOM.

HOW I BUILT MY BUNGALOW

dark walls. The eaves, which have a four-foot extension, are supported by heavy redwood timbers.

Fortunately, my men were most agreeable and willing; in fact, they seemed pleased with every suggestion. I had heard so much about workmen disliking to have a woman "hanging around," that I was, to be sure, happy in finding them so amiable. When I gave an order I stuck to it, and I guess the novelty of a woman who didn't change her mind every minute rather pleased them. I also guarded myself against being "fussy." My foreman often 'phoned for me to come out and explain just how I wanted this or that when he could have gone ahead and finished it up in his workmanlike way and I would never have known the difference. He would go into detail about the various ways of doing the inside finishing, and ask me which I preferred. He was a first-class carpenter; in fact, a cabinet maker, and it all sounded so "pretty" when he told me about it, that I had all the woodwork in the house mitered and finished in the most careful and approved style. Of course, this cost a lot of money, but I wanted my bungalow to be frank and strong and true, so I didn't skimp or economize in anything. I visited the house once a day, usually in the morning, so that I could outline the work for the day if it seemed necessary for me to do so. My husband went out twice a week.

The only real trouble or annoyance I had was with the man who was sent out to do the cobblestone work. He was a foreigner, very independent and very impudent, and two or three times my carpenters, hearing him "boss" me, threatened to throw him bodily off the premises. He insisted that the wall and porch supports ought to be of little stones laid smooth and even, while I insisted that they should be of large stones of irregular sizes laid in the mortar with ends and sides projecting outside the main plaster line. He paid no attention to my wishes, but went ahead, doing exactly as he pleased, mortaring the little round stones together like so many marbles. I realized if this continued the house would be ruined. The first day or two I was too proud to say anything to my husband about the matter. But after laying awake all night I "gave in" and cried out my trouble on his shoulder the next morning. He 'phoned to the contractor who had taken the masonry work, asking him to discharge this troublesome man and get another. I lost no more sleep over the cobblestone proposition, for another and perfectly satisfactory workman was sent me. I was particularly anxious to have a large flat stone on which to put the house number, laid in the mortar in one of the porch pillars, and this man put aside quite a heap of boulders so that I might take my pick. It is such little considerations that make a woman eternally grateful to a workman.

All along the porch wall, and at the tops of the stone piers supporting the rustic porch timbers, I had the mason leave space for flowers, a trough six inches wide and sixteen inches deep. I think this arrangement much prettier, and certainly it is much neater than the ordinary wooden flower boxes, that invariably leak muddy water over the porch floor when the plants are irrigated. I decided on black pointing for the stone work. It brings out the shape and size of every stone, and somehow it gives more character to the masonry, especially where large boulders are used. I had the porch floor cemented and marked off in twenty-four inch blocks, while the ceiling was of narrow wood beading, varnished.

I deliberated quite a bit before settling upon what to use for the exterior walls, finally deciding that split redwood shakes would be best. These called for an inter-wall lining of heavy building paper. Without the latter the house would not be weatherproof. All window and door casings were made of finished lumber and painted green, while the shake walls were stained a corresponding shade. My painter advised two coats of this stain, which consists of paint and distillate mixed in equal quantities, so I bought the material and told him to go ahead. I have since learned, however, that one coat of stain is quite sufficient. By putting on two coats the painter doubled his time check, but I don't blame him. If I had as big a family to support as he has, I might also try to make my jobs elastic. At any rate my house is sufficiently puttied and painted to last for some time.

I had my heart set on a sleeping porch, so incorporated it in the plan. It consisted of a wood platform, 12 x 14, with a pergola roof, and was to be accessible from our bedroom by means of a double

HOW I BUILT MY BUNGALOW

French window. I asked a dealer for an estimate on the canvas for the walls of this sleeping porch. The roof was to be left open, so I could look up at the stars. His bid was $16 for canvas on rollers. This price seemed rather high. After looking about I decided to buy material and sew it and hang it myself. I bought twenty-seven yards of drilling at twelve and one-half cents a yard, the whole coming to a trifle over $3. I measured off breadths for each of the sides, sewed them, and fastened them to the timbers by means of rings sewed to the cloth, and hooks screwed into the wood. I did this so the curtains could be readily removed and laundered. Just now I am having a struggle to prevent the vines which have clambered up the sides, and which are most welcome there as sun screens, from covering the roof. It is such a delight to see the stars the last thing before going to sleep, and the blue sky the first thing upon opening my eyes in the morning.

Floors throughout the house are double. The first, or foundation floor is of six-inch tongue and groove Oregon pine. In living room and dining room the finish floor is of number one quarter-sawed oak, and in the other rooms the finish floor is of white maple. I should never have a maple floor in my kitchen again, for it absorbs the grease in such a way that spots are practically impossible to remove without taking the floor along with them. If building again I would have an ordinary pine floor in my kitchen and give it three or four coats of paint, or better still, cover it with white and green checked linoleum, which always looks clean, even when it is dirty. Adhering throughout to the idea that a bungalow should be low, my ceilings are only eight and one-half feet high. Doors are six feet six inches by thirty inches and are No. 1 grade.

I gave a great deal of time and thought to the interior finish and furnishing of the bungalow. I firmly believe that domestic harmony applies to the things in a house as well as to the people who live in it. An execrable color combination in a room is bound to make one feel out of humor. Furnishings should be harmonious, so that when one comes in tired, one will feel rested and comforted. I struggled and planned and matched things and samples, in an effort to bring about just such a restful result.

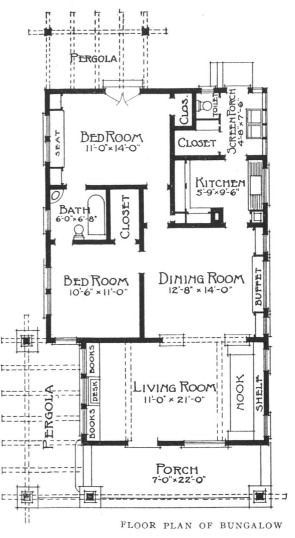

FLOOR PLAN OF BUNGALOW

My color scheme for the living room was brown, with here and there a dash of yellow, ruby and green. I selected two small art-glass windows to go above the mantelshelf on either side of the fireplace. In these were shades of yellow, green and ruby. I got small pieces of this glass from the factory where the windows were made, took them to a wall-paper store, and finally succeeded in finding a narrow frieze in which the colors exactly matched those of the glass. I studied out every little detail in just this same way, even to the glass in the copper and iron electric fixtures. In the living room, bookcases, desk, mantelshelf and buttresses are all four feet high. The paneling ends on the same line, while the square lattice windows are the same height from the floor. Between the paneling and the picture molding, excepting a six-inch space that is given up to the frieze, is a gold-brown wall paper. Above the picture molding, walls and ceiling are covered with deep cream paper. Mantel and hearth are of eight-inch red brick tile, while the hood and twelve-inch facing under the mantelshelf are of hammered copper. I had considerable difficulty in finding tile the right shade. The first lot sent to the house had to be returned. I then went to the shop armed with a bit of copper and a piece of the brown wall-paper, and selected enough red-brown tile of uniform color that blended perfectly with my color scheme. All the woodwork in this room I had stained in imitation of Flemish oak. One arrangement that I find most convenient is that of having a wide, deep box seat on either side of the fireplace, one in which to keep wood, and the in which to keep kindling. They do not leak dirt like baskets, and they hold enough fuel to last a long time. Filling in one entire end of the living room under the lattice windows, is a built-in desk with a bookcase on either side, and now that we are living in the house, we make amusement for ourselves and friends by designating this end of the room as our "library," the central portion where the piano is, our "music room," and the other end as our "living" or "reception room." I fully intended having my foreman make all the furniture for this room, but after he had finished a table, a chair and a foot stool, I found the work, as well as the materials were proving unreasonably expensive, in fact the three pieces cost us $75.00, and while they were beautifully made and finished, I could get just as good in the shops for much less money. I selected a golden-brown bungalow net for the curtains in this room, a color matching exactly the wall-paper.

For our bedroom I chose white paper with white dots—an imitation of dotted swiss, also a cut-out frieze showing garlands of blue roses and green leaves. For the other bedroom I selected a striped paper in white and palest pink-gray. with a cut-out garland frieze of pink roses and green leaves. In both these rooms, as well as in the bath, I had the woodwork finished in white enamel. I planned a built-in arrangement for one side of my bedroom which proves a great blessing. Under the wide window is a roomy box seat with a lid. On either side of this, and fitting into the corners are buttresses thirty inches wide, two feet deep, and four feet high. These have shelves and doors.

In one of them I keep my big hats, in the other my shirt-waist boxes as they come home from the laundry.

I had my kitchen done in cream enamel, even to the furniture, which I bought in the shop unfinished, and had my painter finish it just as he finished the woodwork. For my sink casing, as well as for my drain board and molding board, I selected a cream wood stone. This is better looking, and far more serviceable than the white pine usually used for such purposes.

I had the dining-room woodwork finished to correspond with that of the living room. Under the high windows on the east side of the room is a built-in buffet with shelves and drawers. The color scheme in this room is Delft blue and cream. The furniture is all of white ash of special design. The chairs have woven reed seats.

All the electric fixtures in living room and dining room were made to order from my designs, and while they were somewhat expensive I feel repaid because they are "different."

COST ESTIMATE.

Building permit	$2.00
Water tap	9.00
Cement and stone work, including walks	381.00
Plumbing	190.00
Sewer connection	28.00
Electric wiring	22.00
Electric fixtures	95.00
Lumber	480.00
Doors and windows	116.00
Roofing	90.00
Plaster	75.00
Hardware	57.00
Paint, stain, etc.	90.00
Copper hood, etc., for mantel	30.00
Wall-paper	30.00
Wood stone drain board	12.00
Screens	23.00
Duplex window shades	11.00

LABOR.

Carpenters	540.00
Painter	92.00
Helper	148.00
Floor finisher	12.00
Total	$2,531.00

Since my bungalow has been completed I feel more and more that the building of one's own house is the great step toward reducing this American tendency of moving practically every spring.

A RANCH BUNGALOW EMBODYING MANY MODERN IDEAS: BY CHARLES ALMA BYERS

I T is the exception nowadays for us to build a house in town or suburbs without some, at least, of the modern time- and labor-saving conveniences. We plan for as many bathrooms as we can afford or the size of the family demands; sideboards, bookcases and seats are incorporated into the living room; linen drawers and clothes closets with mirrors set in the doors are planned for the bedrooms, and the kitchen equipment includes a built-in icebox, convenient sink and drainboard, and there must be a compact cabinet that will save time and steps for the housewife.

While these things are considered more or less essential for houses built in more populous sections, it is unusual to find any thought given to the conservation of energy in planning houses for the real country. As a rule, in building a farmhouse the main thing that is considered is the erection of a shelter from the elements, a place to eat in and sleep in, but not necessarily to live comfortably in. It is exceptional to find running water and bathroom facilities in farmhouses, for the drainage problem is one that has to be solved separately for each house, and for that reason is seldom considered at all.

We are accustomed to think sentimentally of the charm of the old-time country house, but when it is compared with the kind of house modern invention has made practical for us, its drawbacks stand out

rather sharply and it becomes less alluring. When the daily round of work and discomfort, the wear of wasted energy are considered, it is small wonder that the youth of our country refuses to see the joys of living in houses that are insufficiently heated, at times badly ventilated, and planned with such lack of thought that it is necessary to take ten steps to do the work of one. Farmers' wives perhaps breathe less pure air than any other human beings, for it takes all day long to do the work of a family and, in this country, the work is all indoors. A walk in the fields or woods holds no allurement for feet that are ready to drop off with weariness, aching with the effort to keep up with the tide of work that never abates.

Life on a farm will never hold interest for those who work too indefatigably to realize its beauties, who never see the sunset because the bread must be baked, and who never hear the birds sing because the work in the pantry must not go unfinished. These conditions prevail to a great extent all over the country, and yet it is not impossible to incorporate modern conveniences in farm homes,—the time- and labor-saving (sometimes even life-saving) features that would make life less a round of drudgery for weary women. Here and there the more progressive of our country folk are demanding for themselves the benefits that the city house affords, and the ranch bungalow illustrated here shows a possibility in this direction. The house is located on a forty-acre ranch or farm, near Burbank, California,

A RANCH BUNGALOW

LIVING ROOM IN RANCH BUNGALOW.

pretentious environment. It is not a small house, as it is 75 feet 4 inches wide and 44 feet 4 inches deep. The front porch is 11 feet by 34 feet 6 inches. One end of the porch is continued into a *porte-cochère*, and the other end is enclosed by one wall of the den. Both the porch and the *porte-cochère* are of massive proportions, and, like the chimneys, walks, steps and porch flooring and parapet, are built of brick. The siding is of cedar shakes, spaced about six inches apart, and stained a soft brown. The roof is of shingles, painted white. There are many windows, mostly casement, and over the front entrance is a series of small dormer windows, set with panes of art glass.

The interior differs most markedly from the old-style farmhouse. There are numer-

and is the home of Mr. J. C. McConnell, a rancher who believes in modern ideas. The house follows decided California bungalow lines, and is modern in every respect. The style and finish, both inside and out, would make it entirely suitable for a city home, and it also deserves especial attention as an example of what can be accomplished in rural home building.

The exterior is particularly attractive,

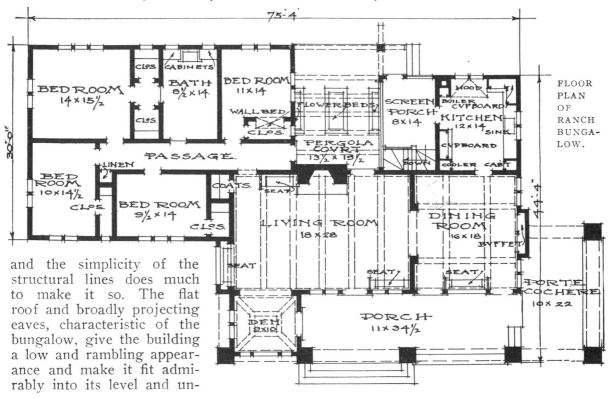

FLOOR PLAN OF RANCH BUNGALOW.

and the simplicity of the structural lines does much to make it so. The flat roof and broadly projecting eaves, characteristic of the bungalow, give the building a low and rambling appearance and make it fit admirably into its level and un-

ous built-in features. In the living room there are three built-in corner seats and a large fireplace with a mantel of pressed brick; the dining room contains an attractive buffet and a comfortable window seat. There are four bedrooms in the house, each with a roomy closet and one with a built-in wall bed, and in the hall there is a convenient linen closet. The bathroom has convenient cabinets, as well as the usual bathroom fixtures, and is 14 feet by 8 feet 6 inches in size.

The kitchen contains ample cupboard space, a draught cooler, an instantaneous heater, a stationary hood for the kitchen range, a sink and a small storage closet. On the small screened porch adjoining the kitchen there are two stationary tubs for washing, and leading from this porch is a stairway to the basement.

Oak floors are used throughout the house, except in the kitchen, bathroom and screened kitchen porch. The ceilings of the living room, dining room and den are beamed, and the walls of these three rooms are paneled to a height of 5 feet, topped by a plate rail. The woodwork, which is of Oregon pine, is finished to resemble Flemish oak, and the furniture has been selected

to match this finish. The upper portions of the walls and the ceilings are plastered and tinted a light buff. The woodwork of the bathroom, kitchen and bedrooms is of Oregon pine, enameled white, and the plastered portions of the walls in the bedrooms are tinted in delicate colors.

One of the most appreciated features in summer is the small pergola in the rear. This is a sort of court, 13½ feet by 19½ feet, enclosed on three sides, and is accessible from both the living room and the hall. It has a cement floor, into which have been sunken spaces for flower-beds. This pergola is furnished with a hammock and rustic chairs, and is an ideal retreat for outdoor lounging.

The house is substantially and warmly constructed throughout. It has a furnace, and is piped for water. The supply of water comes from an elevated tank, and a cesspool is provided for the run-off. The house, complete, represents an expenditure of $4,200, and it ought to be possible to duplicate it in almost any locality for approximately this amount. A. S. Barnes and E. B. Rust of Los Angeles, California, were the architects.

A BUNGALOW BUILT IN SPANISH STYLE IN GLEN-
DALE, CAL., THE HOME OF MRS. J. S. JONES.

A MODERN CALIFORNIA HOUSE OF THE SPANISH TYPE: BY DELLA M. ECHOLS

TYPICAL of the comfort, ease and enjoyment of life that is supposed to be inherent in southern California and its bungalows, is the Spanish residence designed for Mrs. J. S. Jones by a local architect. It is built on one of the beautiful avenues of the suburban town of Glendale, a few miles north of Los Angeles, and is surrounded by wide-spreading pepper trees and other native shrubbery.

This type of dwelling is especially adapted to the southern climate, for all its rooms are spread out on the ground and so are in close touch with out of doors. Moreover, with no stairs to climb, the work of housekeeping is considerably lessened.

The exterior is of sawed shakes down to the water-table, below which are red brick in white mortar. The massive chimney is also of red brick in white mortar. Like all Spanish residences, the roof is flat with a wide overhang about 3½ feet in width, extending the entire distance around the house. This gives the building a much wider

appearance and emphasizes the low bungalow effect.

A great deal of skill is shown in the ar-

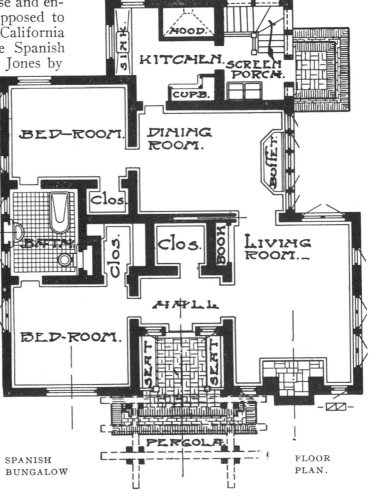

SPANISH BUNGALOW FLOOR PLAN.

A BUNGALOW BUILT IN SPANISH STYLE

FIREPLACE CORNER OF LIVING ROOM IN SPANISH BUNGALOW, SHOWING INTERESTING WALL FINISH.

rangement of the rooms, the idea having been to get the maximum of comfort, convenience and beauty with a minimum of expense. This has been accomplished by a practical and very compact floor plan and by making interest of materials and structural proportions the basis of all decorative effect. There is no attempt at elaborate ornamentation; everything is simple, homelike, designed primarily for household comfort, beautiful because it is appropriate and worked out with artistic feeling.

LOOKING INTO DINING ROOM FROM LIVING ROOM.

A BUNGALOW BUILT IN SPANISH STYLE

From the pergola at the entrance one steps into a hall which separates the living room from the guest chamber. The house is trimmed in natural woods, unmarred by paint and varnish and finished so that one feels the interest and color of the grain. The wainscoting of channel boarding in hall, living room and dining room is 6 feet high. This not only adds to the friendliness and charm of the rooms, but is especially harmonious with the built-in furniture—bookcases, buffet, china closets, etc. These are all constructed on strong, simple lines, and in filling the various needs in a practical way add much to the structural decoration of the interior.

The central point in the living room is, of course, the fireplace, which is built of old gold brick. What a contrast is this "room to live in"—16 x 20 feet—to the cheerless, formal "parlor" of twenty-five years ago! The dining room beyond forms an extension of the living room, and with its combined buffet and china closets is especially convenient.

The kitchen is equipped with all modern conveniences, so that the work of the housewife is more of a pleasure than a drudgery. A very practical feature is the large built-in hood which comes down low over the stove in one corner of the room and carries off all smoke and cooking odors. The kitchen is as cheery in appearance as the other rooms, being all white enameled. A screen porch immediately off the kitchen contains the sanitary laundry trays and also the stairs leading down to the basement, where the furnace is placed.

The bedrooms no less than the living or day rooms are planned for health and restfulness. The windows and doors are arranged so as to provide the best possible lighting and ventilation, while leaving ample space for the beds and other furniture. Access from the bedrooms to the bathroom is easy, and these rooms are conveniently separated from the rest of the plan. The bathroom has a modern equipment, being finished with a tile floor, white enamel woodwork and nickel hardware.

There is one feature in home-building which every woman appreciates, and that is an abundance of clothes closets, particularly the kind that admits sufficient light and air. This plan makes ample provision for such closets. Another factor which adds materially to the beauty of the rooms and helps to lighten the work of keeping them clean, is the provision of hardwood floors. These do not add greatly to the cost, and are certainly worth while, for they permit the abolition of carpets and the use of rugs—both an æsthetic and a sanitary gain. The electric fixtures throughout were designed by the architect, and it is just such attention to detail and careful workmanship evinced in every room which helps to make this little home a place of unusual comfort and loveliness.

The total cost of construction was $2,600.00.

"THE BARNACLE": A LITTLE CALIFORNIA HOUSE MADE FROM A BARN.

THE BARNACLE: TRANSFORMING A BARN INTO A BUNGALOW: BY EUNICE T. GRAY

MY seaside cottage, the "Barnacle," is one of the most successful transformations that I have ever known. In the first place, my sister and I chose, as the site of our cottage, Carmel-by-the-Sea, California, a coast village of unusual beauty and charm. The lots were situated on a gentle seaward slope covered with the sweet smelling Southern wood, rich-hued manzanita bushes, scrub-oak and cascara; two giant Monterey pines with strangely twisted low lying limbs, stood on the seaward side of our lots and a group of smaller pines at the east.

The house completed, faces the east, and the dining-room and living-room windows look out upon beautiful Carmel Bay; the view from the southern windows is the full sweep of the chaparral-covered point between the bay and a small inlet into which the Carmel River flows. This river, in summer, is a placid low-running stream between banks of sycamore and willow; in the winter, fed by the rains and snows it is a roaring flood of mountain wash, rushing through the rich Carmel Valley to the sea. Beyond the river are the foothills, green and wooded, and sloping down to the coast in the long rocky point, called Lobas,

where the rarely beautiful, roseate, abalone shells with their pearly "blisters" are found.

From the upper windows looking eastward we catch a glimpse of the cross of the historic church of San Carlos Mission, founded nearly a century and a half ago.

But in the beginning there was no living room or dining room, for the house like its name began as a barn. It was built four-square, a carriage house, horsestalls, barn-doors and hayloft, painted red and set on the barest corner of the four lots. It cost the sum of eight hundred dollars.

The original barn was twenty-four feet square, built of California redwood, with a shingled gambrel roof, and outside finish of board and battens which we had painted dull red. The lower floor was divided through the center by a partition, which

SHOWING THE RUSTIC GATEWAY AND FENCE.

TRANSFORMING A BARN INTO A BUNGALOW

LIVING ROOM IN "THE BARNACLE."

The upper room was lighted by two east windows and a double dormer window to the south, glass doors opened onto a semi-enclosed west balcony from which we could witness the marvelous sunsets over the bay.

Before the barn was finished we had an opportunity to rent it as a residence to a carpenter who was at work in the neighborhood, so we decided to furnish it simply and comfortably for his family for the winter. We had couches, rugs, linoleum and curtains from our town house which were past their first freshness but still in good condition, these we had shipped down by freight; dishes and kitchen furnishings we bought at the village store; bedding and rag rugs we industriously made, to keep the house as homespun and old-timey as possible. A new stove in the "horse division," a cupboard built of boxes and a work table constituted the kitchen; the carpenter built shelves and a table in the west end, and called it the dining room. The carriage house was converted into a cozy, comfortable living room, with rag rugs, a couch and cushions, a large circular table, two rocking chairs and two low hickory chairs with rawhide seats.

We hung the sides of the upper room with flowered chintz, soft blue covered with roses, the space between this temporary wall and the sloping roof made two long airy closets. We furnished it with cots,

was made by covering the upright beams with heavy gray building paper, on the south side of which an enclosed staircase led to the loft above. Two windows, three feet high and two wide, faced west to the sea, and a door opened onto an uncovered west veranda. The north and south windows were long and narrow, three by one and one-half feet, placed in the exact center of opposite walls.

SOUTH VIEW OF "THE BARNACLE" SHOWING BAY WINDOW AND SECOND FLOOR DORMER.

TRANSFORMING A BARN INTO A BUNGALOW

hickory chairs, dressing-tables made of boxes, patchwork quilts and dull blue rugs. Altogether it was a most attractive room and the wonderful views from the windows were never forgotten by the numerous guests who later occupied the quaint airy chamber.

For two years the new barn, which never housed a hoof or a wheel, was used as a house. We entertained jolly house parties of four to ten in number and the year of the earthquake and fire in San Francisco we found it a safe and quiet refuge from the distress and disorder of the city. The third year we abandoned all idea of building the larger house under the pines and decided to convert the barn into a bungalow. A three-windowed bay was added to the south side, and the second floor balcony, which was found impracticable in stormy weather, was enclosed and made into a tiny bedroom.

The little village had not yet a sewerage system, so modern plumbing was out of the question for that year, at least, but a bathtub was installed in a curtained recess of the living room and a sink and drip-board in the kitchen. The walls of the first floor were wainscoted to within three feet of the ceiling with white pine, waxed and shelacked. The upper portion was covered with linen canvas, and a plate rail was built all around the room. The effect was very artistic and the house was unusually light and attractive. These improvements cost $90.

That summer we rented the "Barnacle" to vacationers through the entire season. They paid $1 a day, and all expressed themselves satisfied with the simple arrangements and comforts of the cottage.

The following fall I bought out my sister's interest in the Carmel cottage and made $300 worth of improvements. With this expenditure all traces of the original barn disappeared; the carriage-house entrance was replaced by pine paneling and three large windows. The "horse door," built in an upper and lower section, was taken out and a very proper door with a pane of glass

and a lock and key was hung in its place.

The old staircase was pulled out and built into the northeast corner, which was now, by the construction of a partition, the front hall; the west end formed a kitchen twelve by eighteen feet. The sink was placed under the long window, and a door was cut on the north side leading onto a covered platform which was used as a woodshed. The east end of the living room is now used as a dining room, and the crowning glory of this long, light room with its beautiful outlook, is a great red brick fireplace with a chimneyshelf and a crane, and a wide hearth and niches on either side for the Chinese bowls and candlesticks. The chimney is not enclosed but rises solidly to the ceiling directly in the center of the house. It has been, indeed, the heart of the house, and when a group of merry friends are gathered about the roaring fire,
"Oft died the words upon our lips,
    As suddenly. from out the fire
Built of the wreck of stranded ships,
    The flames would leap and then expire."
And in those little silent times we experienced true comradeship.

The second floor of the house has received due attention, a bathroom with modern plumbing is the prime improvement, a second dormer was thrown out on the north side and the room finished with pine and divided into three bedrooms.

The rose vines climb over the pergola, and a hardy group of eucalyptus trees rustle their gray-green leaves in the ocean breeze, golden poppies and wild lilac have wandered in from the roadside, and mingle their sweet wild beauty and fragrance with pink geranium and sweet alyssum.

While our architectural methods, as the foregoing account reveals, were certainly unorthodox and unique, both the exterior and interior of our bungalow proved practical and homelike. And perhaps the results illustrated here may inspire some other home-makers to work transformations of a similar nature.

A BUNGALOW OF RARE COMFORT

EXTERIOR VIEW OF MR. E. B. RUST'S BUNGALOW, LOS ANGELES, CALIFORNIA.

A PRACTICAL AND COMFORTABLE BUNGALOW BUILT BY A WESTERN ARCHITECT FOR HIS OWN HOME: BY CHARLES ALMA BYERS

WHEN an architect builds a home for himself it is naturally to be expected that he will create something "different" — something at least not stereotyped. In the first place, no one can interfere with his plans, and in the second place, he can avail himself of the opportunity to put into use many ideas that must have gradually accumulated in his mind. And while practically every architect will allow himself a certain degree of freedom, no matter what style of house he may design, one can expect even more in this way when a Western architect builds for himself a bungalow home.

The bungalow, as has often been stated in THE CRAFTSMAN, probably surpasses all other styles of architecture in its adaptability to individuality. It permits far greater freedom in construction, and makes possible the installation of many more built-in features. In fact, the built-in features of the bungalow have been developed in such interesting fashion and are so necessary a part of the structure that they are a distinct characteristic of this style of building. The bungalow is definitely designed for a home that is both attractive and inexpensive, and to meet these requisites it is essential that the interior be made cozy and homelike without the use of a great deal of expensive furniture. It is here that built-in features are most helpful. They do much toward making the furniture list simple, and at the same time they make possible an interior scheme of furnishing that is harmonious in both color and finish. The immovable fittings of a house are usually built on plain, straight, structural lines, and it is comparatively easy to secure furniture constructed on the same principles and of a finish to match.

The bungalow shown in the accompanying reproductions is an excellent illustration of these facts. It is the home of Mr. E. B. Rust, an architect of Los Angeles, California. Mr. Rust has designed a large number of the bungalows of Southern California which are well known throughout that country, and naturally in his own home one might expect to find embodied some of his best ideas.

As seen from the outside the bungalow is characteristic of its type, but not particularly unusual. Even for the bungalow style it is rather plain and regular in contour, but has pleasing proportions, and, indeed, much of its charm is due to its simplicity. Incidentally, it is gratifying to realize that the age of bizarre architecture is surely passing; that we are being gradually educated into an appreciation of plain, simple and dignified houses

This bungalow has the usual low roof and broadly projecting eaves. The siding

A BUNGALOW OF RARE COMFORT

is of redwood shingles, as is also the roof. and the masonry is of brick. There is a small front porch of well-proportioned lines, and in the rear is the customary screened porch, 6½ x 10 feet in size. The windows are almost all casement, a style that always seems especially suitable for a low-roofed house. The exterior color scheme is two shades of olive brown—a light olive stain for the siding and a darker shade of olive for the trim,—which, with the dull red of the brick, makes a most effective combination.

While the exterior is attractive, the interior shows the skill of the architect to a greater extent. He has given it special consideration. In studying the accompanying floor plan drawing, noting the numerous closets and built-in features and their arrangement, it becomes evident that Mrs. Rust also had considerable to do with their planning. There seems to be "a place for everything," and the location of the various features is so convenient that there could be little excuse for not having everything always in its proper place. And even with so much built-in furniture, a general feeling of simplicity is maintained—a fact which deserves particular mention.

The house contains five rooms, besides a sort of book alcove and the bathroom. The alcove is really a part of the living room, but is sufficiently secluded from the front entrance to give opportunity for the utmost privacy. This nook contains the fireplace, which occupies one corner, three

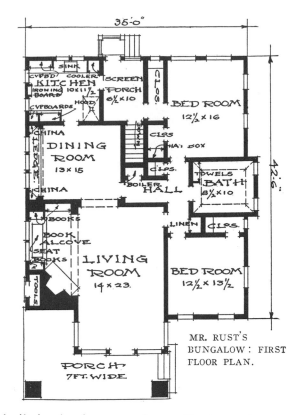

MR. RUST'S BUNGALOW: FIRST FLOOR PLAN.

built-in bookcases of excellent workmanship, and a long comfortable window-seat. The top of the seat is hinged so that it may be lifted as a lid and the box underneath serves as a receptacle for fuel. The fireplace is of brick covered with cement plaster, and the mantelshelf is of wood in plain design. The corner occupied by the fireplace has given an opportunity for a novel feature—a garden-tool closet, which is ac-

LIVING ROOM OF MR. RUST'S BUNGALOW, SHOWING END OF ALCOVE WITH BOOKSHELVES.

A BUNGALOW OF RARE COMFORT

LIVING ROOM, SHOWING THE OTHER END OF ALCOVE, FIREPLACE AND WINDOW SEAT.

ing scheme. The lighting fixtures are particularly interesting and in simplicity of design are quite in keeping with the interior finish and the other features. In the living room the principal fixtures are two large inverted domes of hammered brass suspended on chains, and in the dining room there is a single dome, similarly arranged, made of glass, covered with lacquered bamboo splints. These inverted domes, which hold the electric bulbs, reflect the light against the vaulted ceiling, where it is diffused to all parts of the room in equal strength. In the living room and alcove there are also, at convenient intervals, smaller lighting fixtures of the ordinary kind.

cessible from the outside of the house.

A broad arch, hung with portières, connects the living room and dining room. A rather unusual buffet has been built into the latter. Beneath a series of three large casement windows there is a broad, low ledge, into which have been fitted three capacious drawers. At each end of this ledge, which also means at either side of the three windows, there is a corner china closet, the doors of which contain ten panes of plate glass and correspond in design with the windows.

The woodwork of the living room and dining room, including, of course, the alcove, is of California redwood, which has been waxed, and left in nearly its natural color. This is a very effective wood, and it is impossible to improve upon its color tones. The walls of both rooms are tinted a roseleaf green, and the ceilings which, except in the alcove, are plastered like the walls, are colored a light buff. The ceilings are vaulted, or slightly arched, for the purpose of aiding the indirect light-

To many a housewife a study of the kitchen of this house will prove interesting. This room is finished in white enamel, and is most convenient in arrangement of built-in features. There are numerous cabinets

ONE END OF THE DINING ROOM, SHOWING BUILT-IN CHINA CLOSETS.

A BUNGALOW OF RARE COMFORT

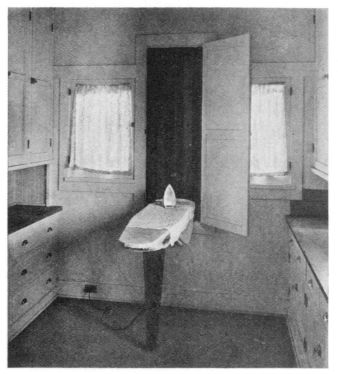

A CORNER OF THE KITCHEN, SHOWING BUILT-IN
IRONING BOARD AND CONVENIENT CUPBOARDS.

and drawers, the usual sink, a hood for the range, a draught cooler, a built-in flour bin, a disappearing bread board, and an ironing board that folds up into its own special cabinet.

There is a roomy closet in each of the two bedrooms, and in the closet of the rear bedroom there is a built-in hat box. On the rear screened porch there is a large storage closet, and in the T-shaped hall that gives access to the bathroom from practically all parts of the house there are two more closets, as well as the boiler cabinet. The bathroom is finished in ivory enamel, and has mahogany towel and medicine cabinets. The woodwork of the hall and the two bedrooms is also enameled, the former in ivory and the latter white, and the walls and ceilings are plastered and tinted in delicate colors.

The house has a small basement, the stairway to which leads from the rear screened porch, and a basement furnace supplies additional heat when that afforded by the alcove fireplace is insufficient. Unlike California's first experiments in bungalow building, the house is strongly and warmly constructed and would be suitable for almost any locality, no matter how severe the winters might be.

Careful attention has been given not only to the more important structural features, but the minor details as well. The interior is satisfying and harmonious in both color and finish, even to the curtain and portière poles, which are made of the same material and with the same straight lines as the rest of the woodwork.

The house has ample ground space, and a few massive old trees that at one time practically monopolized the plot have been given a little pruning, and left to form the basis for a most delightful environment. Home-builders are gradually realizing that such monarchs as these do not grow quickly, and that as a rule it is advisable to plan the house in relation to the natural surroundings. Too often valuable trees are cut down in the mistaken idea that it is necessary to plan the grounds after the house is constructed instead of planning them first. When the house is completed before the grounds are planned and laid out, the builder often learns when it is too late that by the time the garden is mature the house is old and sometimes dilapidated.

HOME OF MR. AND MRS. W. S. JOHNSON, PASADENA, CALIFORNIA: LOUIS B. EASTON, ARCHITECT.

A CALIFORNIA BUNGALOW PLANNED FOR COMFORT: BY LAURA RINKLE JOHNSON

WHEN we purchased our little ranch of five acres on the outskirts of Pasadena, we were very decided as to the kind of house we did *not* wish to build for our home. The problem was to find an architect who would undertake the construction of a well-built, comfortable house, perfectly adapted to the grounds, the surroundings, and our tastes. After some investigation the right man was found in the person of Louis B. Easton.

We were especially fortunate in the location of our property, as in addition to three acres of fine orange trees, there were scattered over the place twelve magnificent live-oak trees of large proportions, some of them possibly three hundred years old. Another advantage was an excellent lawn, formerly used for a croquet ground, closed in on the south—toward the highway—and on the west, by a six-foot hedge of Australian pea-vine. The eastern side of the lawn was filled in with loquat and olive trees. The fourth side of the square was chosen for the location of our bungalow.

The plans decided upon were somewhat on the lines of a Mexican ranch house, adapted to meet the ideals of Craftsman construction, and to conform with the environment. The completed home, a long, low building with an overhanging roof that forms the porch covering, seems just as much a part of the landscape as the oak trees whose branches spread protectingly above the roof.

The materials used in building were Oregon pine and California redwood, the outside being covered with split shakes. These overlap each other eleven inches and the ends were left uneven as cut from the log. There are no "fake" beams or posts in the house, every stick of timber is just what it appears to be, and does just what it seems to be doing.

The porch—fifty feet in length—is an ideal outdoor sitting room. The floor is brick, easily cleaned, and cool on hot days. Four strong pine posts support the porch roof, on the under side of which the construction timbers are exposed. The entrance door of the bungalow we consider most craftsmanlike. In fact, Mr. Easton was so pleased with it when it was finished that he strongly objected to the "sacrilege" of a screen door that would conceal its beauty! However, we now have a screen door, but one especially built to harmonize with its setting.

The natural reddish hue of the redwood is preserved and intensified by a most in-

A CALIFORNIA BUNGALOW-COTTAGE

terest i n g process. Stiff wire brushes are used to scrape the wood, removing all the loose splinters and bringing out the grain of the wood in high relief. A f t e r this treatment the wood is either waxed or given a chemical wash, and the result is most unusual and effective. The metal work on the doors—hinges, latches, etc.—is of iron, copper plated, and was made by a blacksmith near by from designs drawn by Mr. Easton. Throughout the house, the primitive style of latch and handle is used on the doors; the locks consist of a pin of oak, whittled smooth and fastened to the door by a buckskin thong. The pin is thrust above the latch into a fastening on the door casing.

The porch leads into a hall formed by two partitions five and a half feet high, which separate it from the living room, and a wide opening between the partitions forms the entrance into the living room. A group

LIVING ROOM IN THE JOHNSON BUNGALOW, SHOW-ING INTERESTING INTERIOR FINISH AND FURNISH-INGS, ALSO HARMONIOUS FITTINGS.

of four casement windows, with small panes, lights the hall. At the eastern end of the hall is the dining room, and opposite, at the other end of the hall, is a bedroom.

The living room has the real home feeling; its low ceiling and paneled wall spaces, and most of all the spacious fireplace, seem to express our ideal of the spirit of hospitality and simple living. At the right of the entrance is a seat, the back of which is formed by the partition, at right angles to the fireplace. In the fireplace we have tried to express also the spirit of comfort and good cheer we want our home to typify. It is wide and deep, strongly built of red brick, with clinker brick as the only ornamentation; the mantel shelf is a slab of burl redwood, gnarled and knotted; and the hearth of brick is laid in herring-bone pattern.

The partition at the other side of the entrance to the living room offered opportunity for

DINING ROOM WITH GLIMPSE OF LIVING ROOM.

A CALIFORNIA BUNGALOW-COTTAGE

DELIGHTFULLY ARRANGED LIVING PORCH.

group of three casement windows, thus insuring an abundance of air and sunlight.

The chief feature of the dining room is the massive built-in buffet, and much charm is also given to the room by the French windows opening to the east, where we have a fine view of the snow-covered peak of "Old Baldy." The buffet stands between two doors, one leading into the kitchen and the other into the cellar, for, unlike the majority of California bungalows, this one has both a cellar and a furnace.

built-in bookshelves. Opposite the entrance is a group of five casement windows above a broad window seat. The walls here, as in the hall, dining room and sleeping rooms downstairs, are paneled with redwood of strongly marked grain. The space between the wainscoting and ceiling is covered with soft gray monk's cloth; neither plaster nor wallpaper is used in the house.

The ceilings throughout the lower floor carry heavy exposed beams of Oregon pine which convey the impression of great strength. A door leads from the living room into one of the bedrooms on the ground floor. This room is finished much like the living room, and has a door opening into the bathroom, which in turn opens into the bedroom at the end of the hall. Each sleeping room has French windows and a

The kitchen is small, and absolutely no space is wasted. The convenient cupboards, air cooler and work table combine to make the culinary duties less irksome. The kitchen opens onto a large screened porch which is used as a breakfast room.

On the second floor (the stairway leads up from the kitchen) are the guest's room, the maid's room and a large trunk room. The sleeping rooms each contain a lavatory, and in the trunk room a small closet was partitioned off for a toilet. These rooms are finished in the same style as the rooms below, except for the walls, which, instead of being covered with monk's cloth, are paneled the entire height with redwood.

On the lawn, in front of the house, is

COURT BACK OF THE JOHNSON BUNGALOW WHICH FURNISHES OPPORTUNITY FOR SECLUDED OUTDOOR LIVING.

what we call a birds' pool, built from our own design. It is of brick, circular in form, and filled with clear water it affords an opportunity for our feathered friends to drink and bathe. They take naturally to it, and we spend many pleasant moments watching them. Around the pool are planted large elephant's ears and tall stalks of papyrus, and in the water blooms the water hyacinth.

Around the oak tree at the front of the house we laid a brick pavement, and from the porch we can look under the drooping branches of this oak to the nearby mountains.

The buildings at the rear form three sides of a court—a pergola connecting the screened porch with the garage, a small building conforming to the lines of the bungalow, in which are three rooms—a large one for the car, and two smaller ones—a study for the owner and a playroom for the small boy of the family. Extending from the garage is a small building with screened sides, containing a collection of foreign song birds.

Along the rear of the house are planted red geraniums, and roses will soon cover the pergola. A violet bed occupies a favored spot, begonias of various kinds are growing along the front of the aviary, and a banana tree is flourishing in the little court at the back of the house. On the east side we have rose bushes of many varieties and colors, and in a nook is a fern garden, most attractively set among rocks and half-decayed eucalyptus logs. The western exposure boasts a planting of Shasta daisies and climbing roses, and in this land of sunshine a very short time will suffice to produce luxuriant growth.

The electric fixtures of the house are of copper and are made from a design by Mr Easton, to harmonize with the decorative lines in the living room panels.

Our bungalow is livable, homelike, well built, inexpensive and beautiful, to our way of thinking—and more than this no one has a right to demand of a dwelling place.

The possibilities for securing ideal gardens seem greater in southern California than elsewhere, especially in the frostless belt that embraces Los Angeles and vicinity. No flowers have to be disturbed by being taken up for the winter as in the Middle West and East, thus plants attain a larger growth in a single year. The surrounding hills have many wild shrubs and flowering bushes which may be borrowed from them without any damage to their forestry, as some plants, such as the mountain laurels, often need to be thinned out, and these add much native beauty to the home garden, linking it, as it were, with its environment. Then the bungalow is a type of home which seems to come closer to nature than more pretentious buildings, and touches of rusticity are always in harmony with it, and create a feeling of oneness with the land.

A BACHELOR'S BUNGALOW

IF there is a style of bungalow that demands absolute comfort, stability and freedom from non-essentials, it is likely to be that designed for a bachelor. Indeed, the very mention of a bachelor's home in the country conjures up thoughts of freedom, physical comfort and an absence of mundane care. The accompanying plan for such a house emphasizes the intention of solidity in construction, sensibility in design and convenience in arrangements.

That the idea of solidity might be carried out in this bungalow it was constructed of brick, a material well suited to endure and to render the home cool in summer. "Tapestry" brick with wide, rough-cut flush joints face its walls, giving variety and the charm of color to the surface. The same treatment is carried out in the interior of the living room and in the large, welcome-giving fireplace. Again the idea of stability and convenience is presented by the tile floors and walls of both kitchen and bathroom, extending in the former case to a height of 6 feet and in the latter to 4 feet. Here then is nothing in interior wall finish to fade, to wear out or which cannot readily be kept clean and sanitary.

The door frames of all the exterior walls are white oak; other outside trim and shingles being of cypress.

DESIGNED BY H. A. HAWTHORNE.

PERSPECTIVE SKETCH OF BUNGALOW.

SECOND VIEW OF BUNGALOW.

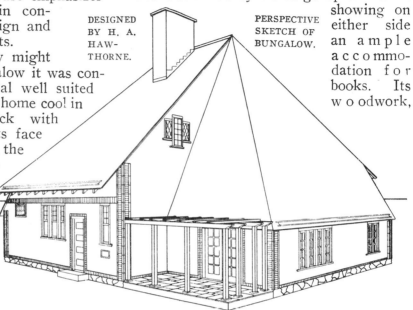

Again the idea of stability is accentuated.

The plan of the house is found sensible in that it utilizes well every bit of valuable space, and in its apparent openness to the outer world. The large living room is open to the roof, affording a sense of space and freedom without which no home in the country lives up to its highest benefits. Moreover, this particular living room is made distinctive by its large open hearth, showing on either side an ample accommodation for books. Its woodwork, stained a walnut brown, harmonizes with the open-air impression of the house, blending well with the brighter colors of nature. The living room opens onto the dining-room porch, which is free to the sky and the sunlight. Should, however, the taste of the bachelor incline toward horticulture, it could be attractively covered, pergola-like, with vines. The pantry and kitchen are so situated as to make service to either the dining porch or the living room entirely simple.

One bedroom is on this ground floor and opens at one end into a commodious bathroom, and at the other onto a recessed porch which might serve delightfully for either an outdoor sleeping room or for an informal breakfast room. The upper half story provides two rooms and a bath, one of which would of necessity be used for a servant. A large cedar closet is in

A BACHELOR'S BUNGALOW

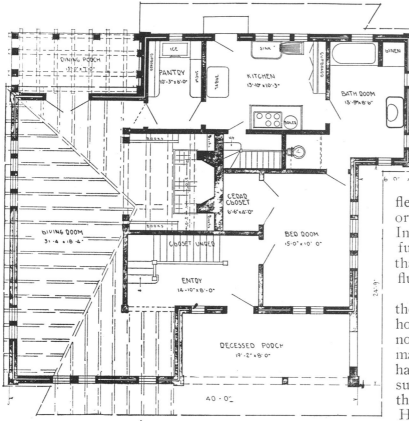

FLOOR PLAN OF BACHELOR'S BUNGALOW.

In this plan of a bachelor's bungalow, the call of the open air life is met. It gives no suggestion of restraint within walls except in places of necessity. Its atmosphere is one of simplicity and freedom. Just as it should be. The owner may have the scout's eye, but it is not for flecks of dust on the shelves or for tarnish on the silver. In his lair, he sees things of fuller meaning, and delights that there is nothing superfluous about.

Should he drop his pipe on the floor, its ashes burning a hole in the carpet, he barely notices the damage. Even it may be that he prefers to have no carpet; the floors are substantial—a rug here and there suits best his fancy. Holding this attitude, the entire furnishings of such a bungalow should be simple in the extreme, strong in outline. They should also be durable, since bachelors invariably expect full service from chairs, tables and other household objects. That furnishings are plain, however, does not in any sense mean that they are crude. They may be made harmonious with the scheme of the bungalow and pleasing as well to the eye. In fact a bachelor's bungalow gives him of all things needful, the opportunity to enjoy his own individuality.

the bedroom, and there is sensible accommodation for linen and household stores.

With the advent of cold weather, the bachelor owning such a home need not be driven cityward by an early cold snap or because the crows have flown over the cornfields with their farewell call. He may rest by his own fireside as late in the season as he chooses, since a Craftsman fireplace makes his home a real shelter from inclement weather. Here he can feel the cheer of warmth and home beside his welcome open fireplace throughout the autumn days. And he can equally well entertain friends over the holidays, knowing that the furnace is substantial and in order, and that it will keep his bungalow from feeling the nip of Jack Frost.

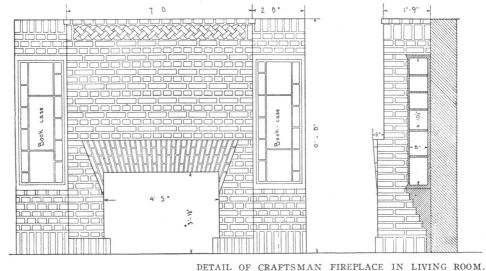

DETAIL OF CRAFTSMAN FIREPLACE IN LIVING ROOM.

SIX-ROOM BUNGALOW BUILT FOR COMFORT

A SIX-ROOM BUNGALOW: IN-EXPENSIVE, COMFORTABLE AND ATTRACTIVE: BY CHARLES ALMA BYERS

THE time seems now to have come when a man of comparatively meager financial supply need be no longer without a home, comfortable and artistic, in which to shelter himself and his family. The six-room bungalow herein illustrated is not only pleasant in its structural lines, but it affords ample space in which to move about, and is planned so as to make housekeeping as simple a matter as feasible. It was built at a cost of only $3,200.

It is distinctively a California bungalow, although of comparatively new interpretation. Its lines, those most suitable for a city home, are straight and regular, simple and dignified. The almost flat roof has at its eaves and gables a broad projection of nearly three feet, its sweep giving to the bungalow an appearance of much greater length and size than it actually possesses. The siding is of redwood shakes, showing about 12 inches of their length; the framing and finishing timbers of Oregon pine and the porch pillars and other masonry work of concrete. Cement forms the floor of the porch, the steps, as well as the paths about the house. The pillars, with their projecting copings, are of massive proportions and are responsible to an extent for the substantial look of this bungalow.

SIX-ROOM BUNGALOW BUILT FOR MR. J. S. CLARK IN LOS ANGELES: HAROLD BOWLES, ARCHITECT.

The arrangement of the front porch may be regarded as a strong point of the exterior. At one end it is enclosed with glass, converting it virtually into a small sunroom, the enclosure being created by a series of casement windows, each one capable of opening when a free circulation of air is desired. The unusual lighting device for the porch is noticed in a modernized Japanese lantern, set on a low pedestal-like pillar, standing at one side of the entrance steps.

The exterior of the house pleases by its apparent strength of construction and its attractiveness is heightened by its color scheme. The roof, a sort of asbestos composition. is white, as is also the concrete and cement work, while the siding and other woodwork are stained in rich brown, causing the whole structure to stand out effectively from the background of green afforded by a line of eucalyptus trees.

In its floor plan this bungalow is particularly commended on account of its convenience, its openness and its built-in furniture. Passing through the front door into the living room it is seen that a screened breakfast room lies beyond, so-called French doors intervening between the two rooms. At the left of the living room is placed the dining room, entered by way of sliding doors, while directly at its rear is a kitchen including as accessories a small pantry and the customary screened porch. At the right side of the living room are located two bedrooms, each with a good-sized

SIX-ROOM BUNGALOW BUILT FOR COMFORT

FIREPLACE CORNER OF LIVING ROOM.

closet, a bathroom supplied with medicine chest and linen closet and the den, the latter connecting with the living room by a broad arch.

A feature not to be overlooked in this plan is the short hall which leads from the end of the living room and connects the two bedrooms with the bathroom. It can be shut off by means of a door so that this section of the bungalow has complete privacy.

Regarding the principal features of the living room, the fireplace first attracts attention since it is large and occupies a sort of Dutch nook in one corner of the room. Its hearth and mantel are of brown tile, while the shelf above is of wood, severe and plain in treatment. Small built-in seats at either end of the fireplace add much to its welcoming sentiment. The room is finished in slash-grain Oregon pine made to look like fumed oak. The floor is also of oak. To hold the room in harmony, the walls, which are of plaster, are tinted a light chocolate brown, the ceiling running off into a delicate buff.

Indeed, the coloring of the room has been commended as more than usually effective.

A large well built-in sideboard marks the dining room, also a commodious window-seat, the top of which is on hinges, in which instance it discloses an appreciable space for storing away various articles. Chocolate-colored leather is used to panel the room to a height of 4 feet, above which a rail is run for holding plates. The upper part of the walls and ceiling, likewise the floor and trim, have been subjected to the same treatment as those of the living room. An ingenious lighting of the room is contrived by art lights concealed in the four corners of the ceiling beams, besides the usual drop light is suspended from the center.

The den, while small, makes a direct appeal to members of the family caring for informality and absolute comfort. It is here that letters are written, there being a built-in desk in one corner, and books read, two bookcases showing against the

THE DEN IN THE CALIFORNIA BUNGALOW.

SIX-ROOM BUNGALOW BUILT FOR COMFORT

walls. The most unique feature of the den, however, is the so-called disappearing bed. This bit of furniture is concealed in the wall between the den and the enclosed end of the front porch, and is so arranged that it can be rolled either into the den or out on the porch. When not in use for sleeping it looks simply like an innocent couch, both from the porch side and that of the den. The finish of the den is similar to that of the living and dining rooms. French doors form for it the means of passing out onto the porch.

ONE END OF DINING ROOM WITH BUILT-IN WINDOW-SEAT AND SIDEBOARD.

FLOOR PLAN OF MR. CLARK'S BUNGALOW.

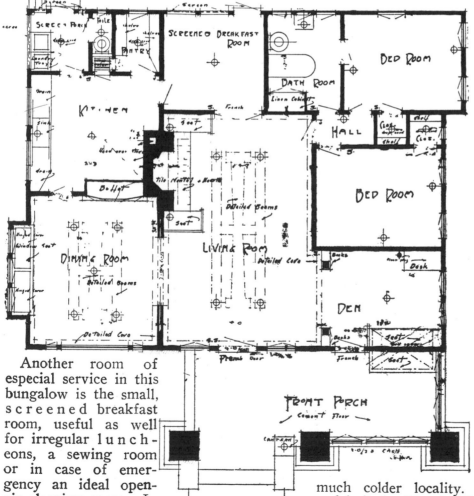

finish and trim it corresponds with the other mentioned rooms.

The kitchen, beside the usual cupboards and closets, is supplied with a draught cooler and a hood for the range. It has the same white enamel finish as the bath and bedrooms.

Although this six-room bungalow is located in a mild climate, where it cannot help but gain much benefit from its porches, its numerous windows and French doors, admitting floods of sunshine and warm, sweet air, it is equipped with a basement furnace, and is in every way so up-to-date in its arrangements that its plan should be feasible in a much colder locality. It was designed and built by Harold H. Bowles, an archi-

Another room of especial service in this bungalow is the small, screened breakfast room, useful as well for irregular luncheons, a sewing room or in case of emergency an ideal open-air sleeping room. In

tect of Los Angeles, California, who is authority for the statement that it could be duplicated in almost any part of the United States for from $3,000 to $3,400, its approximate cost in California. The house is the home of Mr. J. S. Clark.

VACATION BUNGALOWS THAT APPEAL BESIDES AS HOMES OF COMFORT AND REFRESHMENT

WITH the return of summer a longing slips into the heart of men and women alike to be on the wing, as it were, to fly away from the routine of life which occupies regularly the greater part of the year, and in some chosen spot of the earth to refresh themselves by Nature's companionability and to drink deeply of her soothing influences. And somewhere for the earnest man and woman there is waiting a spot, perchance by the sea, at the base of a hillside or near a running stream, where a shelter can be built for the vacation season of the year.

Many, however, are held back from even seeking the bit of earth likely to give them solace, simply because they think they cannot afford to build thereon a home. Their conception of a "cheap house" includes ugliness and inconvenience. Therefore they succumb to the tyranny of a summer boarding-house where the food is often not well cooked or nourishing and where beds are hard and unsympathetic. Later they return to their regular occupations, feeling that disappointment has marred their vacation time.

Probably the most satisfying summer outings are spent in snug little homes, informal places, or at least under a roof where all city-cramped faculties can have full play, for the men and the women who live restricted lives owing to the character of their various occupations above all things crave freedom in their summer outings.

THE CRAFTSMAN has proved that to build a bungalow snug, attractive and comfortable, in full view of the setting sun and where the air moves freely, is not as costly an undertaking as many people suppose. It can be made to come within the means of most home lovers with moderate salaries. If well done in the beginning, it then not only provides a shelter for the summer outing, but a home for all time, paying liberally for itself as time passes. It has always been the ideal of THE CRAFTSMAN to provide men and women of small incomes with homes in which their individuality might be truly expressed, where they

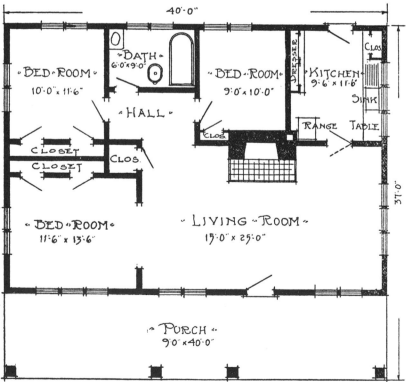

FLOOR PLAN OF CRAFTSMAN BUNGALOW NO. 161.

CRAFTSMAN VACATION BUNGALOWS

CRAFTSMAN SHINGLE BUNGALOW NO. 161: FIVE
ROOMS, BATH AND LIVING PORCH.

might feel themselves in reality a part of their environment.

The two vacation bungalows presented this month by THE CRAFTSMAN make, even through their illustrations, a direct appeal to bachelors, bachelor maids and small families wishing to abide for a while close to the green things of the earth. These houses rest in so friendly a fashion on the ground that they seem to be a part of it. Both are very simple but dignified in character. About them is an air that would attract the interest of anyone seeking peace and joy close to Nature.

BUNGALOW No. 161, the larger of the two, can be built for from $1,500 to $2,000, not a large expenditure when one takes into consideration the completeness of the structure as a home, and the fact that it can be made habitable for the whole of the year should the owner desire.

Sometimes a member of a family may succumb for a time to ill health, when the possession of such a bungalow is of inestimable value. The patient can there regain his health economically in comparison with the charges made at various resorts and sanitariums.

The exterior of this bungalow is covered with shingles. The porch having supports of hewn posts which carry out the idea of harmony with Nature. The roof can be of some sheet composition such as Ruberoid, its slant being hardly sufficient for the use of shingles. When well colored, perhaps by a combination of brown shingles and a green roof, or one of red where a brighter touch is desired, this home appears to fit into the landscape as completely as though it were Nature's own handiwork.

The arrangement of the interior shows this vacation home to be planned so that no space is wasted. From the porch, stretching the full length of the building, one steps directly into the living room with its spacious fireplace opposite the door of entrance. The room is well lighted by the double casements on each side of the door, and by a group of three on the right, so that it will have as much fresh air and sunshine as possible. And as this room and the porch will naturally be the most popular portions of the bungalow, they should be considered in deciding its placing. The best exposure will probably be facing south, giving the living room and porch the eastern, southern and western sunlight.

The living room is a good-sized place—15 by 25 feet—and its size seems increased by the wide openings into the bedrooms on the left and the hall in the rear. If the owner preferred, of course, one or both of these openings might be closed by an ordinary partition and door, or by portières. The east end of the living room can well be used for an informal dining room whenever the inclemency of the weather forbids eating on the porch.

The kitchen directly behind this section of the living room is fitted up along its light east side with a table, sink and drainboard and a closet. The range in the corner of the room uses the substantial chimney for its flue. China closets add to the completeness of the equipment.

This floor plan provides for three bedrooms, each one furnished with a closet, and there is also a large closet in one corner of the living room convenient for coats, or for golf sticks, tennis rackets, fishing tackle, etc. Perhaps only two bedrooms may be necessary, in which case the one opening from the living room may be turned into a study, office, music room or studio, according to the inclination of the home-builder. The two bedrooms in the rear and the bathroom between them open out of the hall, resulting in a certain amount of seclusion for this part of the house, and shutting off at will the living-room section.

More space or more elements of comfort could hardly be gained in a plan of these dimensions. The rooms are well lighted by good-sized windows and the circulation of air is untrammeled.

BUNGALOW No. 162 is considerably smaller than the first one illustrated this month, yet as practical. The cost of its construction need not exceed $1,200. It is built of shingles, field stone and hewn posts, and its roof is sufficiently sloped to permit of the use of shingles, should they be preferred to composition sheet roofing.

As in the first bungalow, the door opens directly from the porch into the living room, and on each side are double casements, while a group of three casements lights the right-hand wall and a single casement is placed on each side of the fireplace opposite. This will ensure plenty of air and sunlight, especially if the bungalow is built, as it probably will be, facing south. While this bungalow occupies less space than the one previously described, its living room is even larger than the first, being 16 by 29 feet. The arrangement of the open fireplace and built-in seats on each side results in considerable structural interest at this end of the room and gives the place an air of comfort and hospitality. We would suggest that these seats be made with hinged lids, for the storage space beneath will be particularly welcome in such a small home. The rear of the floor plan is occupied by

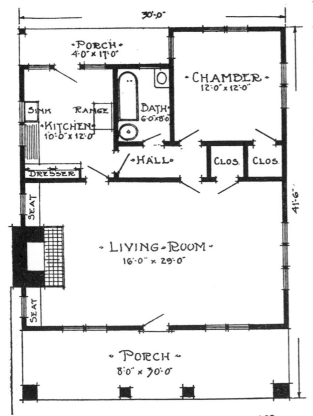

FLOOR PLAN OF CRAFTSMAN BUNGALOW NO. 162.

CRAFTSMAN VACATION BUNGALOW NO. 162: THREE ROOMS AND LIVING PORCH.

the kitchen, bathroom and bedroom, each of which opens out of a small hall, which gives the necessary privacy that is so often lacking in bungalow life. The kitchen is equipped with built-in dresser, sink and drainboard beneath the left-hand windows, with the range opposite where it will get plenty of light from the windows at the back. A door opens onto the small porch, where many of the kitchen tasks may be done in the open air.

The bedroom in the corner will prove particularly comfortable during the summer, for it has windows on three sides that will provide for plenty of cross-ventilation. A good-sized closet is built here next to the one which opens out of the living room.

With thoughts of the spring and early summer wild flowers growing spontaneously about these vacation houses and the asters and golden rods of autumn adding later to their brilliancy, it is hoped that they

will suggest to many ideals of comfortable home life filled with the joy of outdoor living and tranquillity.

In the illustrations of these two bungalows, it will be noticed, we have suggested the use of rustic garden furniture, and in the first sketch is shown a boat-landing with a rustic railing. Other practical suggestions along these lines will be found in an article on page 349, which includes illustrations of various forms of rustic construction—settles and chairs, garden tables, summer houses and pergolas, simple and at the same time decorative in design. Not only do such features invite one to spend as much time as possible in the open air, but they may prove a very effective means of making the little bungalows seem at home among rugged woodland surroundings.

CRAFTSMAN HOUSES BUILT FOR "OUTDOOR" LIVING

THE CRAFTSMAN, in showing in this outdoor number four plans of houses instead of the customary two, does so because it wishes to share with its readers the conviction that the desirable country house of the present is the one that brings the open country nearest to the fireside. This idea is also typified by the two extra plans given this month on pages 322 and 324, which may prove especially serviceable at this season of the year.

For a long time THE CRAFTSMAN has felt that too close and unbroken a home enclosure is not good for the general health of family life, and that all forms of interior stuffiness should be abolished. Moreover, to the fact of living in rooms through which air cannot circulate freely is due, THE CRAFTSMAN thinks, much of the lack of fiber and the physical weaknesses of many people. A superabundance of hangings, innumerable sofa cushions, thick carpets and deep-cushioned seats deprive the individual of the

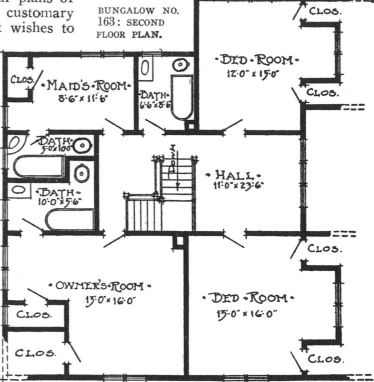

BUNGALOW NO. 163: SECOND FLOOR PLAN.

power to resist the inroads of illness. In succumbing to their influence he forgets his own force. The thinking mind realizes that to live in the open as much as possible is beneficial not only to the body but to the mind, the two together working toward the inevitable weal or woe of humanity.

In planning the two houses shown here, the idea has been to arrange the interiors compactly and economically, and to provide a generous amount of airy, sunlit space while keeping the houses as roomy as possible; in other words, to provide open rooms that have prac-

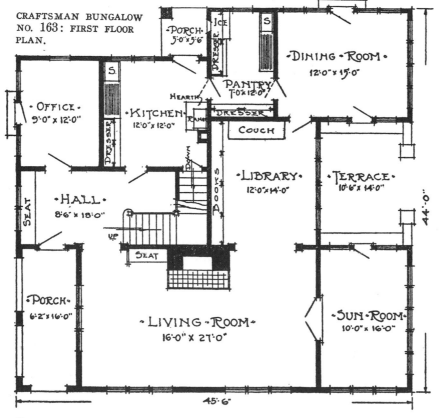

CRAFTSMAN BUNGALOW NO. 163: FIRST FLOOR PLAN.

Gustav Stickley, Architect.

CRAFTSMAN BUNGALOW (TWO-FLOORS) NO. 163: BUILT
TO BRING ALL THE SUN AND AIR POSSIBLE INDOORS.

Gustav Stickley, Architect.

CRAFTSMAN BUNGALOW NO. 164: THE SPECIAL FEATURES
ARE A SUNROOM, LIVING PORCH AND SLEEPING PORCH.

tically the value of porches and yet are a permanent part of the living area.

HOUSE No. 163, a two-floor structure of cement with a roof of asbestos shingles, while presenting an exterior different from most Craftsman houses, has lost neither simplicity nor dignity; it has nevertheless gained considerably in power to open up freely to the outside air, and to draw within its shelter the beauty and freshness of the garden.

The lower walls of this house are made up largely of casement windows, which can be thrown open readily to flood the interior with sunlight and air. The windows of the sunroom can be completely removed during the warm weather and their place taken by screens. This generous amount of windows and the way in which they are grouped together is one of the most interesting and unique features of the exterior. Moreover, they give the house an appearance of close relationship with nature, so that even indoors one will not feel shut away from the odor of flowers and the sweet smell of the earth.

In order to emphasize this wholesome idea of opening a house well to the out-of-doors, we have illustrated the east side of this dwelling, the morning sun bathing it early and working gradually around to the south, where it suffuses the sunroom, living room and entrance porch.

This porch can be better seen in the plan than in the perspective view. From it one steps into a hall lighted by double casements, beneath which the long window-seat is built. The woodwork of the staircase, which turns up to the right, may be made an attractive part of this hallway, and if it seems advisable to have a coat closet here one might be built in the corner between the stairs and kitchen. The arrangement of the hall will be found particularly convenient, as it shuts off the kitchen from the main living portion of the house. It also insures privacy for the room which we have marked "office," and which may, of course, be put to whatever use is most desirable for some busy member of the family.

From the hall one passes into the living room, which will prove an unusually light and cheerful place, with its many windows, its open fireplace and built-in seat, around which the furnishings will naturally be grouped. From this room two glass doors give access to the sunroom.

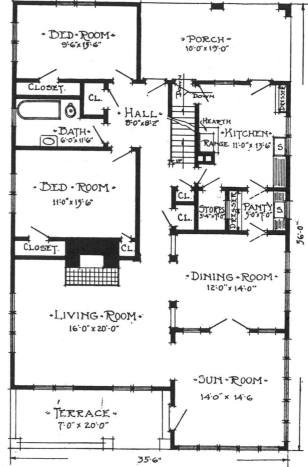

CRAFTSMAN BUNGALOW NO. 164: FLOOR PLAN.

This sunroom should naturally hold no furniture or floor covering likely to be damaged by a whimsical shower or by a rough wind driving the leaves from the trees through its open spaces. It depends, moreover, upon the inclination of the owner whether or no the glass windows, with the passing of cold weather, are replaced by screens or blinds, also a good deal upon the location of the house. If situated in a section of the country free from mosquitoes, Japanese blinds would be preferable, as they can be lifted up when not needed for shade, leaving no hindrance to the entrance of air. In this sunroom, away from office, entrance porch, hall and their traffic, one may find secluded comfort and shelter. Flowers, vines, and other plants could be grown in this room, making it almost into a conservatory.

From the sunroom one steps through a glass door flanked by windows down onto the terrace, which, while sheltered by the walls of the house, is open overhead. This terrace is raised a little above the garden level, and an additional air of coziness is given by low cement parapets and posts. The latter offer just the places for pots of flowers—nasturtiums would give rich patches of color—while in the corners of the terrace against the walls, tall potted shrubs might be set. The terrace floor might be of cement, unless a note of warmth and variety were preferred in the shape of red brick tiles.

Overlooking the terrace are the windows of the library, which opens out of the living room, and in this light pleasant place we have indicated bookshelves lining the long wall and a couch against the shorter partition.

Nearby is the dining room, which is built practically like the sunroom, with its walls almost entirely of windows and glass doors opening to the terrace and garden. In winter this room will be glassed in, while in summer screens may take the place of windows, converting it into an outdoor dining room or porch.

A good-sized pantry with two dressers, sink and ice-box separates the dining room from the kitchen and the latter connects with a small porch from which the ice-box may be filled.

The second floor plan will be found especially convenient. There is a large central hall lighted by three windows overlooking the terrace; the two bedrooms on this side of the house are irregular in shape on account of the dormer construction, and on each side of the dormers are closets beneath the slope of the main roof. These dormer alcoves can be made very inviting by the building of window-seats. For these two bedrooms a bathroom is provided at the head of the stairs, while the rest of the second floor is taken up by the owner's room with its two large closets and private bath, and the maid's room and bath.

IN order to carry out properly the scheme of House No. 164, it should be built facing the south, for this will insure plenty of sunlight for the many windows of dining room, sunroom and living room. While this house is very different in layout from its predecessor, all the rooms being on one floor, the same principles are used in the general construction and arrangement of the sunroom.

The lower part of the building is of brick, the upper part and chimneys finished with stucco, while the roof is covered with asbestos shingles. This combination gives variety of texture and lends itself to an interesting color scheme. By way of contrast with the red brickwork, asbestos shingles of a soft green might be chosen; brown woodwork would look well with the natural-colored stucco, while a lighter note might be added by painting the door and window sash white.

The charm of this house is its nearness to the garden and its homelike coziness. The terrace offers the means of entrance and is enclosed by a low parapet topped by boxes in which flowers are planted. These and the flower-boxes at the sunroom windows bring the garden and house into such intimate companionship that one hardly knows where one leaves off and the other begins. To keep these boxes filled with flowers that show bloom during the months that the house is occupied, flowers rich in color and alluring in fragrance, at once becomes a delightful occupation for one member of the family. When the house is lived in throughout the year, as will most likely occur, the plants of summer's gay bloom can be replaced in the autumn by evergreens able to stand cold, harsh weather and to lift themselves in their cheerful dress of green above the whiteness of the snow. It is at this season that the glass windows, on which the sun shines freely, warm the room with an electrifying glow obtainable from no other source.

A couple of steps from the terrace lead up to the sunroom, which, if made cheerful with plants and comfortable with willow furniture, will prove an entrance at once unique and inviting. A wide opening leads to the living room, which is lighted by casement windows and warmed by an open fireplace, and on the right, separated by post-and-panel construction, the dining room is found. From this room glass doors with windows on each side lead to the sunroom, and as there is also a group of three casements on the right it will prove an unusually light and interesting place for the serving of meals.

Behind the dining room are the pantry and kitchen, the latter opening on to a large sheltered porch at the rear, where many of the kitchen tasks may be done during the warm weather. If this porch is surrounded by a parapet it could even be used for sleeping purposes, as it is convenient to the bedrooms and bath. The attic may be used for storage or it may be finished off as a maid's bedroom.

MORE CRAFTSMAN BUNGA-LOWS FOR COUNTRY AND SUBURBAN HOME-BUILDERS

A S the months go by we are having more and more requests for simple bungalow designs—five- and six-room homes, suitable for suburban or country sur-roundings, with the kind of plans that will combine homelike comfort with economy of c o n s t ruction. A n d especially these prospective h o m e - builders want all their rooms on one floor, so that one maid can do the w o r k e a s i l y; while in many cases the arrange-ment must be so simple that the housewife c a n dispense with out-side help alto-gether.

We have al-r e a d y designed and published in THE CRAFTSMAN a g r e a t many bungalows along t h e s e practical lines, but there seems almost no limit to the possi-bilities of variety i n bungalow planning — not variety m e r e l y for its own sake,

but to meet different local conditions and different family needs. And so, realizing that the more designs we publish, the more helpful we can be in aiding our friends to select or work out their own ideal plans, we are presenting two more this month.

If we have overestimated the popularity of the one-story bungalow, and many of

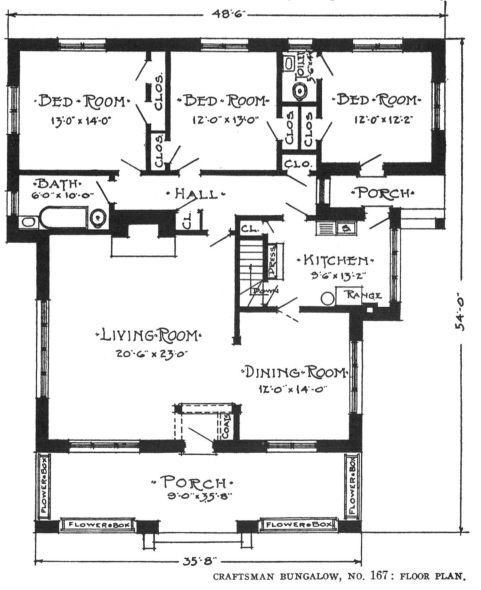

CRAFTSMAN BUNGALOW, NO. 167: FLOOR PLAN.

Gustav Stickley, Architect.

SIX-ROOM CRAFTSMAN BUNGALOW OF FIELD STONE, WITH
LONG PORCH AND COMPACT HOMELIKE INTERIOR: NO. 167.

100

Gustav Stickley, Architect.

FIVE-ROOM CRAFTSMAN BUNGALOW OF STONE AND SHINGLES, PLANNED FOR SIMPLE HOUSEKEEPING: NO. 168.

BUNGALOWS WITH LARGE LIVING ROOMS

our readers are interested in other types, we shall be only too glad to hear from them personally, so that in future we may work up other plans that will be useful to them. For the more closely we get in touch and the more familiar we become with the needs and ideals of those whom our magazine reaches, the better able we shall be to help them through its pages in molding those ideals into realities.

The bungalows illustrated here are planned for country spots and will look equally well among the woods or mountains, beside a lake or stream, or near the shore. They may be built for summer homes and furnished with a few simple, durable belongings, or they may be built and furnished to live in all the year round. Probably most people will prefer to use them for permanent homes, as they are roomy and well equipped, planned for the greatest possible family comfort both for indoor and outdoor living.

While especially adapted, as we have said, to a more or less rural environment, many home-builders whose occupations make it necessary for them to be within easy reach of the city, may prefer to build these bungalows on suburban lots. And in this case we would lay emphasis upon the need of care in choosing the location; for such low, simple dwellings as those we have pictured here will not appear to advantage unless the houses around them are very similar in style. Needless to add, the more garden space there is, and the more rugged and irregular the ground, the greater possibility of achieving picturesque results.

The plan of the first bungalow, No. 167, was worked out for one of our clients who

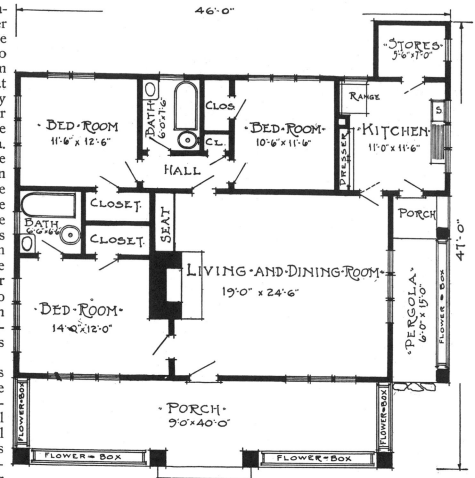

FLOOR PLAN: CRAFTSMAN BUNGALOW NO. 168.

wanted us to design him a summer home. There is plenty of field stone where he intends to build, and as he is particularly fond of this material he decided to use it as much as possible in the construction. Accordingly, we have shown stone walls and stone pillars for the porch, with shingles in the gables and roof.

If others wish to build from this design and field stone does not happen to be available in their locality, brick, concrete or shingles may be used instead. If built of brick, either brick or wood pillars would be most appropriate for the porch; if of concrete, square concrete posts or turned wood columns would be in keeping; and if of shingles, hewn log posts would add to the rustic air. In any case, we would suggest that the gables be of different material from the main walls, to give a little variety and to emphasize the low effect of the exterior.

The porch floors are of cement, and we have indicated wooden flower-boxes between the pillars, as they will give a little privacy and will help to link the house and garden together.

From the front porch one steps into a small vestibule which provides a place for coats and screens the rooms from draughts from the front door. The living room is well lighted by groups of small-paned casements on two sides, and there is plenty of room for comfortable chairs and settles to be grouped about the open fireplace at the farther end.

A wide opening on the right leads to the dining room, which, although only 12 by 14 feet, will be quite large enough for a family of three or four people and their guests.

The kitchen is just behind, with the cellar stairs on the left beside the built-in dresser, and a broom closet in the corner. The sink and range are not far from the windows, and a door at the rear leads out onto the small porch from which the maid's bedroom opens. The latter is large and well lighted by windows on two sides, and in addition to the closet there is a private toilet. This arrangement separates the service portion of the bungalow from the rest, giving the maid her own little home, as it were, secluded from the family rooms.

It will also be noticed that the arrangement of this narrow porch permits the placing of a window in the right-hand end of the long hall which separates the family bedrooms and bathroom from the rest of the plan.

As the space beneath the roof is merely ventilated by louvres in the gables and is not intended to be used for storage, we have provided as many closets as possible —two small closets in the hall, two in the middle bedroom and a single long one in the room on the left.

It would be a good plan to install a Craftsman fireplace in the living room of this bungalow, for this would keep the rooms at a comfortable temperature during much of the spring and fall without lighting the cellar furnace.

THE second bungalow, No. 168, is not quite as large as the first, and is entirely different in arrangement and construction. We have shown the walls covered with shingles, the roof with composition sheet roofing, while field stone is used for the foundation and end pillars of the front porch, as well as for the chimneys. For the pillars on each side of the entrance, however, we have used wood, for this forms an intermediate link between the textures of the rough stonework and smooth roof. Wood pillars are also used for the

pergola porch at the side. As in the preceding bungalow, we have indicated flower-boxes between the pillars, set on the cement floor.

The entrance door opens directly into the big main room, which is living and dining room combined. A coat closet may be provided across the right-hand corner, and if the owner prefers to have the entrance nearer to the closet and farther from the fireplace, the arrangement of the front windows and door may be reversed.

A fireside seat is built in on one side of the chimneypiece, and this end of the room will naturally be furnished as a general living room, while the dining table and sideboard will be placed over toward the right, near the kitchen.

The pergola porch at the side will be a convenient place for outdoor meals, for it is accessible from the kitchen. The latter has windows at the side and rear, which ensure plenty of light at the range and sink; a long dresser is built on the left, and there is a large closet for stores at the back, lighted by a window on the side.

If the owner wishes to build this bungalow with a cellar, the right-hand portion of the plan may be excavated and the kitchen rearranged to make room for the stairs. In this case the laundry may be in the cellar; otherwise, wash trays may be placed in the kitchen, or the closet at the back, which we have marked "stores" may be used as a laundry and a door arranged to open directly into the back garden.

The bedrooms should prove especially convenient, for they afford that privacy which is so desirable in a one-story home. The owner's room, large and light, with its private bathroom and big closet, opens out of the living room, while the two other bedrooms are separated from the rest of the plan by a small hall.

The bungalow, as it stands now, would be suitable for a small family, where the mistress wished to do her own work; but it could be readily adapted to accommodate a maid by making the right-hand rear bedroom open from the kitchen instead of the hall.

IN building the two bungalows which we have shown here, the question of the exterior color scheme will naturally be an important one and will depend on the nature of the landscape or neighboring houses and the owner's taste. If the first bungalow is built of field stone, as we have shown, the varied tones of the stone will give interest of color and texture to the walls and porch, which may be brightened by light green flower-boxes, door and window trim and white sash. A deep moss-green in the gables and reddish brown for the shingles of the roof will be in keeping, especially if the building is set among woodland surroundings.

The second bungalow will probably look well if the shingled walls are stained light golden brown and the roof is olive green. The trim and flower-boxes may also be green and the sash cream or white.

THE EVOLUTION OF A HILLSIDE HOME: RAYMOND RIORDON'S INDIANA BUNGALOW

UCCESSFUL home-building implies something more than the selection of a desirable site, the drawing of suitable working plans and the erection of a practical construction. It implies a sympathetic use of building materials, an understanding of that harmony which should exist between the house and its environment, between the exterior construction and the interior finish and furnishing, between the character of the house and the characters of those who are to live in it. And perhaps more important than all, it implies a genuine home-seeking, home-loving spirit. For the factor that determines the architectural, and one might almost say spiritual, success of such an undertaking is the vision that guides the architect's pencil and the builder's tool, the ideal that inspires the home-maker in the working out of his plans, from the general scheme down to the smallest detail. The house he is building is the house of his hopes and dreams, probably the fruit of long years of work and study and contemplation; its erection means the fulfil-ment of a long-cherished plan; it is to be a home for his soul as well as for his body, a little corner of the world that is essentially his own. This vision, this ideal is the "north star" which guides the successful home-builder safely into his desired haven.

It is just such hopes and dreams, you feel, that must have inspired the planning and building of the house shown here—the home of Mr. Raymond Riordon, Superintendent of the Interlaken School at Roll-ing Prairie, Indiana. Whether you view it from the lake, the garden or the clover-covered hillside, or whether you step inside its sheltered porch and hospitable rooms, you feel instinctively that it is a real home, planned by those who knew by heart the country, the materials and the needs of the people who were to live therein, and who had studied out, thoughtfully and lovingly, how to make the building fulfil those needs in the wisest and most beautiful way.

Seldom have we encountered a more interesting example of utility and beauty combined, and seldom have we seen a house that was more at home among its surroundings. Nestling there snugly against the gently sloping shore, with the log schoolhouse, dormitory and other school and farm buildings clustered around it, the hill of white clover and the young apple orchard nearby, this brick and clapboard bung-alow raises its many-windowed walls, shingled roof and sturdy chim-ney, an embodiment of architectural peace.

THE CRAFTSMAN HOME OF RAYMOND RIORDON, SUPERINTENDENT
OF THE INTERLAKEN SCHOOL AT ROLLING PRAIRIE, INDIANA

ONE END OF THE LIVING PORCH IN MR. RIORDON'S HOME,
WITH A GLIMPSE OF THE SLEEPING PORCH BEYOND.

A CORNER OF THE SHELTERED SLEEPING PORCH IN MR.
RIORDON'S HOME OPENING FROM ONE OF THE BEDROOMS.

FIREPLACE NOOK IN THE LIVING ROOM OF
MR. RIORDON'S BUNGALOW.

A CORNER OF ONE OF THE BEDROOMS, WITH
SUN AND AIR THE FIRST CONSIDERATION.

IN WORKING OUT HIS OWN PLANS FROM THE ORIGINAL CRAFTSMAN DESIGN, MR. RIORDON INCLUDED THE LONG SPACIOUS "ATTIC" LIVING ROOM, TWO VIEWS OF WHICH ARE SHOWN ABOVE.

AN INDIANA HOME ON CRAFTSMAN LINES

Behind the house an excavation has been made and a red brick court built with a retaining wall eight feet high, edged with cement flower-boxes and broken by an entrance of brick steps leading down to the kitchen door. Above the kitchen steps is a pergola, and the projection overhead, seen in the photographs, is a rainwater box with a pipe leading to the kitchen basin. This rainwater box contains a steam coil which keeps it warm in winter and free from frost—one of the many instances of practical forethought in which this home abounds. In addition to this, the kitchen is piped, of course, for hot and cold water.

In front of the house is a flower-bed which was planted with a thousand tulips—and one can easily imagine what color glory their bloom must have lent this woodland spot. When their reign was over, the bulbs were taken out and heliotrope planted in their stead to form another link in the garden's circling chain of color and fragrance.

On one side, facing the faculty house, the hill was planted with crabapple and cherry trees, while on the slight slope from the wall to the brick court, vivid peonies bob out in all colors, ready for the picking. In the shadow of the slope and sheltered by these lordly neighbors, modest lilies-of-the-valley raise their white blossoms among the green; toward the ice-house stand the friendly hydrangeas, ready to follow the tulips, peonies and geraniums with their lavish bloom.

On the lake side, the steeper slope is closely planted with flowering currant, spirea, buckthorn, syringa, and here and there a cluster of bright tiger lilies flashes on the eye. A winding path leads to the boat house, where canoe, rowboat and sailboat nestle on runners ready to slide out for pleasure or for rescue.

The rear of the house is massed with shrubs and cherry trees, and here one finds the rose garden, where hundreds of varicolored blossoms scent the air and add to the beauty of the hill.

And all this gardening was done, all this expanse of plant life propagated, protected and cared for, by boys —mostly by one little boy of twelve!

THAT brings us to the most delightful feature of this lakeside bungalow—the fact that it is not only the home of the superintendent, but also a club house for the boys and teachers of the school community of a hundred and seventy people. And surely, this bungalow is an ideal gathering place for the inmates of such a school — a school that aims to develop body and mind in wholesome harmony.

Turning to the plans and illustrations, we find that the design was adapted from a certain five-room, stone and shingle Craftsman bungalow, published about three years ago in THE CRAFTSMAN Magazine. And it is interesting to note how carefully and at the same time with

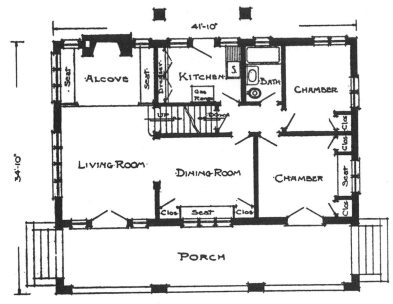

MR. RIORDON'S BUNGALOW: FIRST FLOOR PLAN.

what pleasing originality the owner and his assistant architect, George W. Maher of Chicago, have adapted the Craftsman plan to meet the special needs of individual and site.

The main floor plan of "Number Ninety-three" was carried out practically as we had drawn it, and to it were added a basement and second story. The changes in the elevation and the detail on the second floor were drawn by Mr. Maher from specifications which Mr. Riordon furnished, and between them they have certainly managed to achieve an unusual and satisfying result.

The front entrance is through the long porch which extends across the entire front of the building and is divided into a "sitting porch" and a sleeping porch, the former opening into the big living room, the latter into one of the bedrooms. Some idea of the substantial comfort and cheerfulness of the arrangment can be gathered from the photographs which Mr. Riordon has sent; for as he remarks in his letter to us, "Photographer Koch has made his lenses do effective work."

Stepping from the porch into the living room, one is greeted by the welcome sight of a big, comfortable fireplace nook, where built-in seats and bookshelves with curtained windows above add to the interest of the rough brick chimneypiece and tiled hearth.

The dining room with its wide opening is nearby, so that it seems almost a part of the large main room, and its wide windows frame a generous view of the lovely countryside.

The rest of the floor comprises a small hallway which serves to shut off the kitchen from the dining room and also separates the two bedrooms and bath from the rest of the house.

The woodwork of the interior is especially interesting, for its simple construction and mellow finish evince the real craftsman spirit, filling the rooms with an atmosphere of peace and dignity that reminds one of the quiet forests from which the timber came. Oak flooring is used throughout, and oak is also the finish of the living room. Downstairs all the rest is birch, upstairs yellow pine.

AND now we come to the "attic." We put it in "quotes" because the word loses, or rather outgrows, its usual meaning when applied to such a room as the one pictured here. No dingy, cobwebbed place is this, tucked away beneath the rafters and breathing that strange, musty odor which shrouded in mystery the attic that our childhood knew. No—the term has acquired a new meaning, now that we have seen the photographs of Mr. Riordon's bungalow home. For this is an attic of distinction, comfort and charm.

You climb the staircase that leads up beside the fireplace nook, and find yourself in the center of a long, well lighted room with simple and inviting furnishings—long cushioned seats beneath the curtained windows, willow armchairs and roomy settles, handy tables and shelves where books and magazines lie temptingly about, and best of all an open fireplace, with andirons upon the hearth and faggots that need only a match to start a crackling blaze. The rugs upon the polished oak floor, the shelved closets built against the walls beneath the sloping roof, the lamps for table, wall and ceiling which at nightfall shed their soft mellow glow about the room — all these things contribute to the general air of comfort and loveliness.

The room is large enough for sixty-five boys to enjoy its hospitable spaces, lounge around among the seats and cushions, bury themselves in books, indulge in rest or study, serious debate or idle chat as the spirit moves them. And one cannot help thinking how jolly and companionable it all must be, what a spirit of comradeship such hours must bring to teachers and students alike. Unconsciously one remembers the inscription above the chimneypiece downstairs, *"To Teach Boys to Live"*—and after all, to what finer purpose could any man dedicate his home?

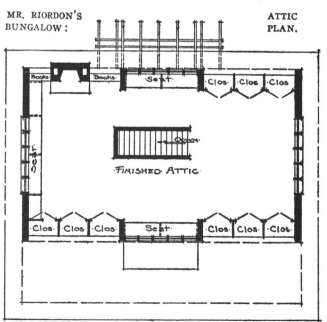

MR. RIORDON'S BUNGALOW: ATTIC PLAN.

A WESTERN BUNGALOW IN WHICH ECONOMY AND BEAUTY MEET: BY H. L. GAUT

THERE seems no end to the variety that an architect can get out of that apparently simple combination—four rooms and a bath. At any rate, the designer of the California bungalow shown below seems able to achieve originality with each small home that he undertakes, and undoubtedly his success is due to the fact that he works out the plans in close sympathy with the needs of the owner and with due respect to the limitations of the site. And in striving thus for the greatest possible amount of practical comfort within a restricted space and income, he gains an unusually picturesque and satisfying result.

In this low-roofed, many-windowed little home we find much that is charming. The simple and effective use of cobblestones, concrete and wood has made a very attractive entrance, and the addition of ferns on the posts and in the window-boxes has added to the friendly air. The floor plan is full of thought for the convenience of those who live and work there, and the arrangement of the woodwork, built-in

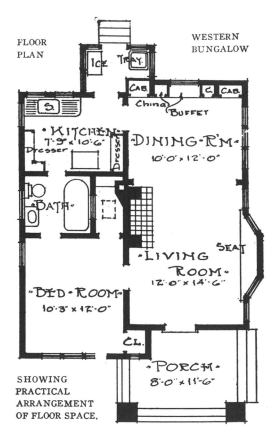

FLOOR PLAN

WESTERN BUNGALOW

SHOWING PRACTICAL ARRANGEMENT OF FLOOR SPACE.

A WELL PLANNED BUNGALOW

A BUNGALOW SHOWING INTERESTING COMBINATION OF WOOD, STONE AND CEMENT.

fittings and other structural features suggests how much substantial beauty can be embodied in even so inexpensive a dwelling.

One of the most interesting points about this bungalow is the grouping of the windows in the right-hand wall of the living and dining rooms. As a glance at the plan and exterior will show, this wall is practically of glass, so that plenty of light and air is insured for the interior. The bay window of the living room is made doubly inviting by the building-in of a seat, and one can imagine how readily both rooms must lend themselves to simple and artistic furnishing.

The fireplace of course is an important feature, and as it is built in the center of the left-hand wall, its warmth and cheery glow can be enjoyed from both rooms; besides, the division between them is so slight that the effect is of one long room extending the depth of the bungalow.

The layout of the kitchen and bedroom on the left with the bathroom between and accessible from both, is especially compact and utilizes the given space to the best advantage.

DETAIL OF BUNGALOW REVEALING EXCELLENT ROOF LINES.

113

A CRAFTSMAN BUNGALOW WHOSE OWNER WAS HIS OWN ARCHITECT

OUR mail is full of pleasant surprises, and not the least delightful among them recently was the unwrapping of the bungalow photographs which are reproduced here. For although we receive many pictures of houses, Craftsman and otherwise, from all parts of the country, few of them have proved more charming than this little Michigan home. Therefore, knowing that every successful house holds innumerable suggestions for other builders, we decided to share the views in question with our readers.

Perhaps the best way to describe the building of this bungalow is to let its owner, Mr. William F. Freeman, tell the story in his own words, which he did very simply and clearly in his letter to us.

"Here," he said, "are some Kodak pictures of a bungalow I have built for myself —not from any particular Craftsman plan, but from ideas gained through reading your magazine. We first determined what our requirements were, made a list of them, and then started to plan around them. I made my own drawings, and while they were somewhat crude, the carpenters had little trouble in grasping my ideas.

"The bungalow contains a living room, dining room, two sleeping rooms, bath-

BUNGALOW AT GRANDVILLE, MICHIGAN, THE HOME OF MR. WILLIAM F. FREEMAN, PLANNED ALONG CRAFTSMAN LINES BY THE OWNER, WHO WAS HIS OWN ARCHITECT, SUPERINTENDED THE BUILDING AND DID MUCH OF THE ACTUAL WORK HIMSELF.

room, kitchen, pantry, coat room and entrance hall on the main floor. There is a large attic, which will be divided into three rooms later. The good-sized basement contains a water-heating system and a gas-engine-driven water system. I did all the plumbing and electric wiring, drove my own well, installed the water system and also the water-heating system. In this, however, I had to have the assistance of a steam fitter, as the weather was getting cold and we had to hustle it in, which we did in six days. The other work was done during evenings and holidays, extending over the whole summer.

"We built a shack for a kitchen and slept in a tent that we might be on the ground and watch the builders—for the bungalow was put up by day labor. Considering that we did not have the services of an architect, we think ourselves lucky in getting the results we have, and we feel greatly indebted to THE CRAFTSMAN for many ideas.

"We find the bungalow a very convenient place in which to live and work, and when we finish our grading, planting and the many other things that remain to be done, we believe it will be a thoroughly successful home."

There is something curiously stimulat-

BUILT HIS OWN CRAFTSMAN HOUSE

A VISTA THROUGH THE BUNGALOW INTERIOR, SHOW-
ING THE USE OF POST-AND-PANEL CONSTRUCTION AND
SMALL-PANED WINDOWS.

ing, inspiring even, in the sort of thing that this home-maker has accomplished. It reminds one of the spirit of the old pioneer, the feeling of adventure which is really at the root of all constructive work, although we have most of us lost sight of it in our ready-made civilization. Many of us would like to do just what Mr. Freeman has achieved; but we are afraid to trust our own skill and judgment. We feel the need of professional architects, contractors and builders. It is so much easier to turn things over to others than to work them out for ourselves.

Of course, this is necessary to a great extent, for most of us have no time to give such an undertaking the study and attention it demands. We cannot compete with experts who have years of specialized training behind them. But when a man *can* work out his own plans, hire his own labor, pitch his tent right there on the ground to see that the work is done as he wants it done, and even take off his coat, roll up his shirt sleeves and do a good deal of it himself—he will find that the results amply repay those efforts. And not the least of his benefits will be the joy he has tasted in tackling the work at first hand, coping successfully with difficulties and molding gradually into tangible shape the home of his heart's desire.

Besides, an experience of this kind has a definite technical as well as spiritual value, and is by no means to be despised as a factor in

the development of skill as well as character. The man who has the brains and ingenuity to do his own plumbing and electric wiring, to paint his own porch and stain his own interior trim, may well be proud of his achievement, for it shows that civilization has not robbed him of manual dexterity and that he is not ashamed to dig and plant in his own little Eden in order later to reap the fruits and gather the blossoms of his toil. We all know the charm of an inglenook and the comfort of our "ain fireside"; but how many of us know the pleasure of sitting beside a chimney-piece that we ourselves have built?

The exterior of the building, with its simple lines, its use of rough stone in the chimney and pillars of the entrance porch, the low roof lines, overhanging eaves, and long dormer, all show the same simplicity and frankness which characterize Craftsman designs.

Indoors, too, one finds the same practical and attractive use of structural features, such as the inglenook with brick chimney-piece, built-in bookshelves, high windows above, and plain wood settles on either side.

Certainly Mr. Freeman has the happy faculty of culling from many designs the principles and features which please him, and applying them to his own needs in a natural and serviceable way. For in this little bungalow one feels no sense of "patch-work architecture." Its most evident quality is that of repose. And planted there in the woodland landscape, it seems the very embodiment of homelike peace.

INGLENOOK IN THE FREEMAN HOME, WITH BRICK FIREPLACE,
BUILT-IN BOOKSHELVES AND SEATS.

A NEW ZEALAND BUNGALOW THAT SHOWS THE TRUE CRAFTSMAN'S ART

"IF a craftsman is to be successful he must base his efforts on essential principles. He can only be sure of himself after years of study and deep seeking. In other words, he must discover the relation of art to human life. With this rock for his foundation, he may speak, through the medium of wood and brick and stone, the truths that have come to him."

There is much wisdom in this simple statement of a craftsman's creed, and it is lent all the more weight because it comes from the pen and heart of one who has sought to embody its meaning in concrete form. It is the expression of a successful architect, a man who has himself thought and studied much, who plans and builds not only with due consideration for those who are to occupy his dwelling, but also in keen sympathy with the materials beneath his hand. He respects the individuality of each—and incidentally, in doing so, expresses his own.

The result, as the accompanying photographs show, is a building of sturdy charm, stamped, in spite of its simplicity—perhaps because of it—with a certain rare distinction that one does not meet in every bungalow. It is quaint, but not eccentric; unique, but not affected; fashioned with frank intention of material comfort, yet imbued with an atmosphere that is far from materialistic. For the spirit of home is there—the brooding quiet, the sheltering friendliness that comes with simple walls and solid woodwork, pleasant windows that gather air and sunlight, and furnishings that invite to sociability and rest.

The fact that this architect, Mr. J. W. Chapman Taylor, is a New Zealander, and the bungalow in question was designed and built by him for a family in New Plymouth, New Zealand, gives an additional interest to these illustrations, for it shows how wide and all-pervading is the architectural *zeitgeist* of today. This new home-building spirit, with its yearning for comfort, for simplicity and beauty, for sincere and earnest craftsmanship, is by no means limited to America and the countries of the Old World, but is stretching out into other continents and colonies and inspiring pioneers beyond other seas. It is infusing into a craft which modern industrial methods have commercialized, somewhat of the old-time ideals that guided the builders and artists and cabinetmakers of long ago. It is forsaking the cult of the machine-made and the gaudy, and hailing the rebirth of a half-forgotten art.

One cannot glance at these pictures of "Plas Mawr," this New Zealand bungalow, without feeling an echo of the home-ideals and the enthusiasm that must have gone into its conception and making.

NEW ZEALAND HOUSE IN CRAFTSMAN STYLE

Even the exterior, with its plain, light-reflecting walls, its casement windows nestling beneath the eaves, its broad sheltered entrance and sloping roof, suggests the unpretentious comfort and the artistic restraint one finds within. And the neat, inviting grounds with their well kept lawn, cobblestone wall with pergola above the walk, and fernery at the farther end, all hold a promise of vine-clad loveliness. For the house, one must remember, is a new one, and the garden has not yet had time to soften with foliage and blossoms the boundary line between art and nature.

IT is interesting to read the architect's description of this bungalow and see how he adjusted plans and materials to meet the needs of owner and site. The lot, it seems, was a triangular one, with its long side to the street, and the "motor house" and boundary wall were already built of river boulders laid in cement when the planning of the house was begun. The space being limited, the problem was to place the house so that while the rooms had sun and view the remaining ground would be left as much as possible in one broad piece.

The material chosen for the walls was ordinary building brick laid as smoothly as possible on the inside and roughcast outside to keep out the damp. The roof was covered with green slates, a few purple ones being introduced here and there to vary the color and surface—a plan that had already been adopted in the "motor house," and the repetition of which brought the two into harmony. Under the roof a large attic room was provided, twenty-eight feet long and twelve feet wide, with cupboards and a built-in window-seat to add to its convenience.

The ceilings were plastered between the beams, and the surface worked to a suitable texture with a brush while the plaster was still wet. The whole interior was distempered white, forming a pleasant contrast with the rich dark-colored jarrah wood of the trim, which was oiled and waxed. Concrete flags were used for the floor, laid on dry sand with cement-pointed joints, and small red tiles were set at the corners to give a brighter note. The floor was well waxed so that it would be pleasant to the tread and easy to keep clean.

For the structural timber work and the furniture, both movable and fixed, the jarrah wood was adze-hewn, mortised and tenoned together and fastened with wood pins, the heads of which project slightly, giving a decorative touch while adding to the effect of strength. In fact, the furniture is constructed on the lines followed by the old wagon-builders of England. It is strong, comfortable, with a certain primitive art that comes of itself when simple tools

"PLAS MAWR," A MODERN BUNGALOW OF UNUSUAL CHARM DESIGNED AND BUILT BY J. W. CHAPMAN TAYLOR, ARCHITECT, FOR MRS. C. H. BURGESS, NEW PLYMOUTH, NEW ZEALAND.

LIVING ROOM AND INGLENOOK WITH CRAFTSMAN FIREPLACE IN THE NEW ZEALAND BUNGALOW: A PLACE OF UNPRETENTIOUS CHARM THAT SHOWS IN EVERY DETAIL THE TOUCH OF SYMPATHETIC ARCHITECT AND CABINETMAKER.

A GLIMPSE INTO THE DINING RECESS OF "PLAS MAWR," REVEALING THE SIMPLE BEAUTY OF THE ADZE-HEWN WOODWORK AND THE RESTFUL ATMOSPHERE THAT PERVADES THE HOMELIKE ROOMS.

A BEDROOM CORNER IN THE BUNGALOW, WHERE CHINTZ CURTAINS ARE USED WITH PICTURESQUE EFFECT: THE CASEMENT WINDOWS AND CURTAINED DOORS ADD TO THE DECORATIVE INTEREST OF THIS DAINTY INTERIOR.

and human handiwork are employed. On seeing it one instinctively contrasts it with the modern machine-made type; for although the machine, by performing many mechanical operations such as the cutting of mortises, boring of holes or making of joints, can relieve the cabinetmaker of much labor, it can never form a substitute for the hand and spirit of the worker.

Realizing this, the maker of the woodwork and furniture for this bungalow, instead of using the planing machine to smoothe the surface of his wood, chose the more primitive adze, which gives to the surface a look of unevenness that lends individuality and charm. It brings out, moreover, the knotty, irregular nature of the wood, its odd little twists of grain, all those intimate, inherent qualities that remind one of the tree of which it was originally a part. As the architect of this bungalow has fancifully put it, "Even though our beams come to us mill-sawn, there is a better and more beautiful beam inside the sawn one; and it is this that the adzeman reveals when he hews away those parts which the blind machinery has left overlaying the beauty of the tree—just as the sculptor releases with his chisel the statue reposing in the marble block."

This principle, as Mr. Taylor reminds us, applies to all materials, from brick to jewels, and it was kept in mind during the designing and making of every detail of "Plas Mawr." Each part bears the impress of an individual hand, from the white-washed walls to the pottery on the mantelpiece.

It is particularly interesting—to us, at least—to discover in this bungalow many evidences of its owner's study of Craftsman designs. The post-and-panel construction between the rooms that lends such airy spaciousness to the interior; the frank treatment of each structural feature; the solid proportions and plain yet satisfying lines of the furniture; the elimination of unnecessary trim or ornament, and finally the Craftsman fireplace that strikes such a homelike note in the living-room inglenook—all reflect in their own fashion the source from which they were drawn.

Whichever way one turns something original and delightful greets one, whether it be the touch of brick in the window sills, the cushioned seats built around the walls of the dining recess, the chintz curtains and lamp-topped posts of the bedroom or the flower-filled vases that brighten table and shelf.

Yet with all the art that has been woven into this bungalow interior, there is no displeasing self-consciousness, no straining after the unusual or extreme. Whatever is unique and surprising seems rather the result of spontaneous enthusiasm and natural feeling for picturesqueness, ready sympathy with the materials, eagerness to make even the commonest detail a thing of loveliness.

THE COTTAGE-BUNGALOW

COTTAGE-BUNGALOW: A NEW DEVELOPMENT IN INTIMATE HOME ARCHITECTURE: PHOTOGRAPHS BY HELEN LUKENS GAUT

THE cottage-bungalow is the newest development in the small American home. We are presenting in this article two designs for this most interesting and intimate variety of domestic architecture. As is the case in many very practical ideas in modern building, these houses have been built in California, yet in spite of their perfect adaptability to the climate there, they furnish us throughout the eastern section of America a most valuable inspiration for home-making. The California architect, Sylvanus B. Marston, has, as examination of these floor plans shows, been able to combine the best points of the simple, old-fashioned cottage and the more elaborate and modern bungalow idea.

In working out this interesting and successful experiment—which may have been quite an unconscious one on the part of its originator—Mr. Marston has chosen from each style those characteristics which are most in keeping with modern American ideas of home comfort, health and beauty. He has retained the simple, sturdy, democratic air of the cottage, with its suggestion of solid indoor comfort and wholesome living; at the same time he has combined with it the airy porches, the ample living rooms, friendly firesides and craftsmanlike woodwork and fittings of the bungalow. And while placing most of the rooms on the ground floor to save unnecessary housework and stair-climbing, he has also utilized the space beneath the roof for sheltered open-air sleeping.

The result is a new type of intimate home architecture which is likely to prove wide in its appeal. And as it is capable of endless modification to meet the diverse tastes and requirements of different families, and the demands of varying climates and environments, the cottage-bungalow should prove a fresh inspiration for the home-builders of our land.

Two examples of this style of dwelling are illustrated here, both of them revealing a practical and sympathetic treatment of design and plan. They bring together, in an original and delightful way, the most desirable traits of the cottage and the bungalow. Neither word alone would accurately describe them; their qualities can only be expressed by employing both. The low long roof lines, the wide eaves, the placing of the main rooms on the ground floor, would seem to assign the buildings to the bungalow category. Yet the construction of the walls, porch pillars and

COTTAGE-BUNGALOW IN PASADENA, CALIFORNIA: A NEW TYPE OF DOMESTIC ARCHITECTURE WHICH COMBINES MANY PRACTICAL AND CHARMING FEATURES: COST OF CONSTRUCTION $4,000: SYLVANUS B. MARSTON, THE ARCHITECT, HAS ACHIEVED HERE AN UNUSUALLY SATISFYING EXTERIOR AS WELL AS PLAN.

121

THE COTTAGE-BUNGALOW

pergola are suggestive of Colonial cottages. But whichever influence predominates, they are certainly satisfactory "hybrids," and will be found worth studying, for they have been arranged and built for real comfort, pleasure and durability. Their compact simple layout, moreover, will appeal to housewives who wish to dispense with the services of a maid.

THE cost of construction of the first cottage-bungalow was $4,000. Its walls are of pearl-gray siding with white trim; the chimneys are dark red brick, and the roof is covered with moss-green shingles. The ventilators in the roof, the heavy barge-board molding at the eaves, the curved group of small-paned windows at the front, and the inviting recess of the porch

room is especially attractive with its open fireplace and small windows on either side, while a seat fills the curve of the bow window, flanked by built-in bookcases. In the dining room, buffet and china closets extend across one wall with windows above.

The arrangement of pantry, kitchen and screen porch is unusually practical, for the space is utilized to the best possible advantage, and is shut off from the rest of the plan. A small hall off the pass pantry gives access to cellar and attic stairs, and in this hall a coat and a broom closet are provided. The long hall at the left communicates with the three bedrooms and bath, which are thus separated from the remainder of the house. One of these bedrooms has a door onto the screen porch, however, so that it may be used for a maid, if necessary.

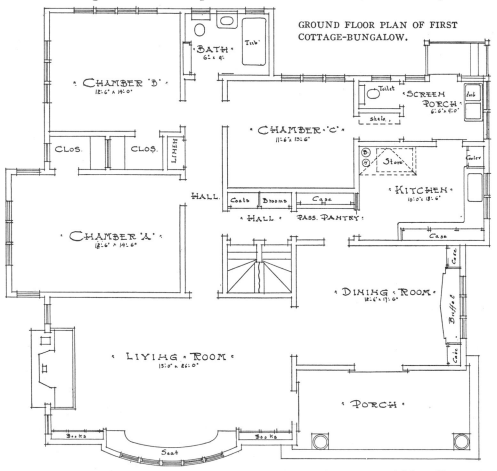

GROUND FLOOR PLAN OF FIRST COTTAGE-BUNGALOW.

are all interesting structural items. A decorative note is added by the wooden frame for vines on each side of the window group.

The building is 45 by 46 feet in area. The plan shows a very convenient arrangement of living and dining rooms, which open from the front porch. The former

Although one would hardly guess it from the front view, there is considerable space beneath the roof of this cottage-bungalow, which is lighted by windows in the gables and in the rear roof. In the latter, moreover, is an extension which makes full head room possible. This gives space for a large screen porch and dressing room up-

THE COTTAGE-BUNGALOW

SIMPLE YET DECORATIVE EXTERIOR, AND COMPACT, HOMELIKE ARRANGEMENT WITHIN, MAKE THIS COTTAGE-BUNGALOW IN PASADENA WORTH STUDYING: COST OF CONSTRUCTION $3,500: SYLVANUS B. MARSTON, ARCHITECT: THE ARCHED ENTRANCE AND PERGOLA-ROOFED PORCH ARE PARTICULARLY INTERESTING.

stairs, increasing considerably the sleeping accommodations and value of the house without adding much to its cost.

THE second house required even less outlay—$3,500—for it is somewhat smaller, having only two bedrooms on the ground floor. And while the style of the building reminds one of the first, it is quite different in plan. The exterior is provided in this case with a long porch across the front, the central part roofed and arched gracefully to shelter and emphasize the entrance, and the space on each side being of open pergola construction.

This cottage is 43 by 40 feet, with 14 by 16 cellar and concrete foundation. Heat is furnished by fireplace and furnace. The outside walls are of resawed redwood siding, painted dove gray, and the trim is white. Out-swinging lattice windows are used, and the entrance door, with its long narrow windows, is heavily cased, with curving bracketed top following the lines of the hood. The interior woodwork is of straight-grain Oregon pine, kitchen and bath being all in white with hard plastered walls and enameled woodwork.

The living room is large, with pleasant window groups and open fireplace, and the dining room with its built-in buffet and china cabinets is separated from the other room merely by bookcases and posts. In this cottage-bungalow no pass pantry is provided, but a small hall separates the kitchen from the front of the house. A screen porch with laundry tubs is built beyond. The two bedrooms and bathroom are also shut off from the other rooms by a hallway from which the cellar and attic stairs ascend. Upstairs are two sleeping porches and a dressing room, all built under the rear raised roof.

These cottage-bungalows furnish, moreover, interesting examples of that significant feature of modern home-making—the architectural solution of the servant problem. For many years we have been growing more democratic in our ways of building as well as in our manner of living. American women have been coming to feel that a large house and several servants are luxuries that have a superficial rather than a genuine value. Many have begun to discard elaboration for simplicity, to prefer a small, comfortable home to a large preten-

THE COTTAGE-BUNGALOW

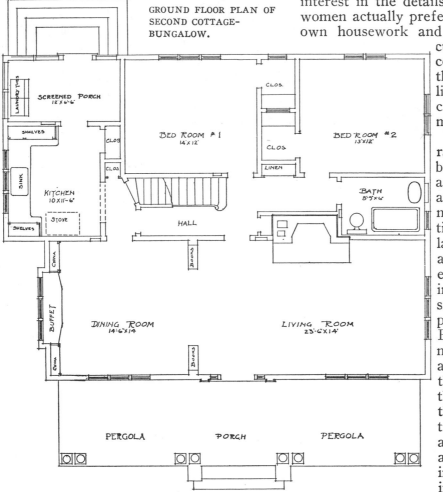

GROUND FLOOR PLAN OF
SECOND COTTAGE-
BUNGALOW.

interest in the details of the home. Some women actually prefer to do much of their own housework and cooking. The difficulty, too, of procuring competent helpers and the higher cost of living has brought increased interest in domestic channels.

These things, naturally, are gradually being reflected in our architecture. Homes are being planned to meet the new conditions. The wide popularity of the bungalow and cottage types is evidence of the growing desire for the small, intimate, compactly planned home. Elimination of all needless halls, passages and stairways, to save the housewife's steps; the simplifying of all the woodwork and fittings to make dusting and cleaning as light as possible; the building of many furnishings, such as sideboards, china closets, bookcases and seats, as integral parts of the interior to reduce sweeping and moving to a minimum—all these features are part of the general and wisely democratic trend.

tious one, and to plan their hospitality on an informal instead of a formal scale. This change of attitude toward essential things has naturally brought about a simplification in household management, a more personal

COMFORT AND ECONOMY COMBINED IN SMALL CRAFTS- MAN HOMES

O NE of the greatest charms of most old-fashioned dwellings—Colonial homes, for instance, or English farm or manor houses—lay in the generous size of their rooms, especially the main or living room. They were built in the days of large families, and before the concentrative energies of modern civilization had made men measure real estate by the square foot instead of by the acre. Today, many of our home-builders, particularly in the suburbs of the larger cities, find themselves confronted with the problem of obtaining the utmost modern comfort in a moderate-priced house on a narrow lot—and it sometimes needs considerable ingenuity to devise a plan which will utilize the available space to the best possible advantage.

One difficulty in planning a small cottage or bungalow is to provide a sufficient number of rooms in the limited area given, and yet prevent the interior from seeming cramped and small. It is desirable that a feeling of openness should be insured above all for the living and dining rooms, since this part of the house is sure to be the most used. A practical and pleasant way to accomplish this is to have the two rooms communicating with each other, with a wide opening between them. In the Craftsman bungalow and cottage which we are showing this month, we have introduced a variation of this

method which may offer a timely suggestion to those of our readers who are planning homes. We have made the division between the rooms even less than usual, so that they have substantially the effect of one long room. A study of the plans will show just how this has been done in each case, and will reveal a compact and economical use of space throughout the rest of the interiors. The arrangement of rooms should make the housework comparatively easy.

FLOOR PLAN OF CRAFTSMAN SHINGLED BUNGA- LOW NO. 201.

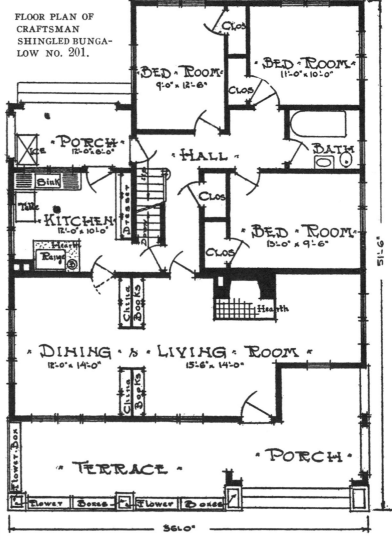

Gustav Stickley, Architect.

CRAFTSMAN SHINGLED BUNGALOW NO. 201: THIS SIMPLE, COMFORTABLE HOME HAS BEEN PLANNED TO MEET THE NEEDS OF A SMALL FAMILY, AND COULD BE BUILT ON A NARROW SUBURBAN LOT: THE ATTIC SPACE MIGHT BE FINISHED OFF FOR MAID'S ROOM, GUEST CHAMBER OR NURSERY, AS DESIRED.

Gustav Stickley, Architect.

THIS TWO-STORY CRAFTSMAN HOUSE, NO. 202, IS BUILT WITH THE LOWER WALLS OF STUCCO, AND SHINGLES IN THE GABLES AND ROOF: THE FLOOR PLANS, ON THE OPPOSITE PAGE, SHOW AN UNUSUALLY COMPACT AND ECONOMICAL ARRANGEMENT OF THE INTERIOR.

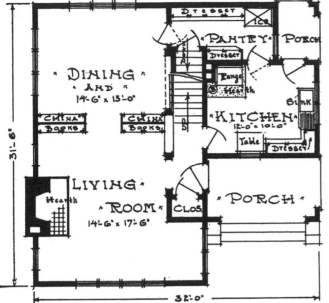

CRAFTSMAN CONCRETE AND SHINGLE BUNGALOW NO. 202: FIRST FLOOR PLAN.

THE first design that we are presenting here is a bungalow, No. 201, planned for a small family of moderate means who wish to combine real home comfort with simplified household arrangements. The building is particularly suitable for the suburbs, and being only 36 feet wide could easily be placed on a 50 foot lot without crowding too close to possible neighbors.

The shingled walls and roof have been kept fairly low, both for economy of construction and to emphasize the homelike air of the exterior. Rough stone is used for the foundation and chimneys, to give a note of variety in texture and coloring, although brick would accomplish the same result if stone did not happen to be available in the locality where the bungalow was built.

The entrance is especially inviting, for one steps up onto a sheltered porch, one corner of which is cosily protected from winds by the walls of the living room. The parapet on the right, and the arrangement of pillars and roof, make it possible to enclose the space by screens in summer or glass in winter. A terrace extending across the rest of the front also provides a pleasant space for open-air life, separated a little from the garden by the low stone wall and flower-boxes between the small brick posts—a device which makes the outlook from the dining and living room windows very pleasing. Brick has also been used above the stone steps of the porch.

As the roof of the porch shelters the front door, no vestibule is provided, so that you step directly into the living room and are greeted by the welcome sight of the big open fireplace with its tiled hearth. At the right of this is a sort of alcove off the main room, with two casements overlooking the garden at the right and another on the recessed porch. The rear wall of this alcove provides an appropriate place for the piano, while the music cabinet could stand either beside the chimneypiece or in the front corner.

As we have indicated on the plan, this room and the dining room are practically one, for the division between them consists merely of low cabinets, with shelves for books on one side, and for china on the other. The dining end of the room has a group of three casements in the front and side walls, and as there is no projecting porch roof except at the entrance corner, the place will be light and sunny, especially if the bungalow is built facing south. If the owner prefers to have the entrance at the left-hand side, and the morning sun in the dining room and kitchen, this can be attained by simply reversing the plan. Another modification, which some people might desire, and which would probably be necessary in a cold climate, is the utilization of the recessed corner of the front porch for a hall or vestibule. In this case, of course, the entrance door would be arranged here instead of where indicated at present.

The idea being to keep the bungalow as simple and economical as possible, no pass pantry has been provided; the kitchen,

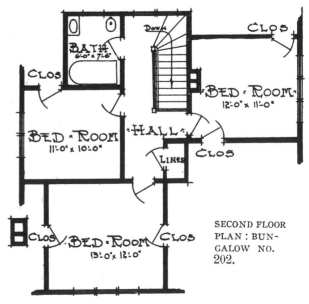

SECOND FLOOR PLAN: BUNGALOW NO. 202.

though only 12 by 10 feet, is quite large enough for a dwelling of this size, and the range, dresser, sink and work-table are well-lighted and convenient. The ice-box is on the service porch, which is so constructed that it can be screened or glassed in, according to the season.

In the center of the bungalow is a hall which affords convenient communication between the front and rear, and separates the sleeping rooms from the living portion of the house. From this hall, also, descend the cellar stairs, with those to the attic just above, and a closet for coats or linen against the opposite wall. If the three bedrooms and bath on this floor did not afford sufficient accommodation, the space beneath the roof, which is lighted by windows in the gables, could be finished off and used for maid's room, guest chamber or nursery, according to the family needs.

THE second design, No. 202, shows a two-story cottage, with the lower walls of stucco, and shingles in the gables and gambrel roof. If built with the living room facing south or east, plenty of sunlight will be insured for this room and the dining room. The entrance is well sheltered by the angle of the walls, and the living room is further protected from draughts by the small passage or hall, with its coat closet, which is arranged here. This hall also gives access to the stairs, and permits one to answer the front door bell from the kitchen without passing through the other rooms.

The same type of combined living and dining room is shown here as in the preceding house, and the arrangement of the groups of casement windows and open fireplace adds to the decorative interest as well as comfort of the place. The staircase is partially screened from the dining room by a grille and from the living room by a half-height partition with a shelf for ferns or pottery, giving an opportunity for an effective use of the structural woodwork. A pass pantry with two built-in dressers and an icebox forms the communication between dining room and kitchen, and from this pantry the cellar stairs descend beneath the main flight. In the kitchen, the sink and work-table are placed beneath windows, and a dresser is built into the corner between. A small recessed porch is provided at the rear.

The second floor has been planned so as to obtain three bedrooms with full-height ceilings, and plenty of closet space is provided beneath the slope of the roof. There is also a linen closet in the hall.

WHAT TWO THOUSAND DOLLARS WILL ACCOMPLISH IN BUILDING A COMFORTABLE HOME: BY CHARLES ALMA BYERS

Photographs by the Author.

IT has often been declared that an attractive house need not cost any more than an unattractive one. This seems especially true of the bungalow, for there is no type of building that lends itself more easily to economical and at the same time beautiful construction. Our California architects, particularly, have proved this in their many successful designs. They seem instinctively to appreciate the decorative possibilities of their materials. In the exteriors they use brick and stone, cement, shingles and timbers, always in a way that brings out the natural beauties of texture, coloring and form. And in the design and finish of interior woodwork and structural features, they work along equally simple and artistic lines. In the arrangement of the rooms, too, they evince a delightful originality without being at all eccentric, and by solving each problem from an individual standpoint they manage to achieve a remarkably distinctive and homelike result. And all this they accomplish at a surprisingly reasonable outlay.

The home-builder, therefore, who seeks economy as well as comfort, finds it worth while to study California bungalow plans,

THE BUNGALOW HOME OF MR. R. H. DREW, LOS ANGELES, CALIFORNIA, DESIGNED BY E. B. RUST, ARCHITECT, AND COSTING ONLY $2,000.

and the one presented here serves as an excellent illustration of the principles that underlie most of the buildings of this general type.

This charming little five-room home cost only $2,000 to erect, and when one notes its many admirable points one wonders how it could have been built for such a comparatively small sum; for it is not only pleasing in appearance, both outside and within, but also substantially constructed and well equipped.

In style it has all the characteristics of the Western bungalow—a roof that is almost flat, wide eaves, rough sturdy timbers, and generous window groups. The outside walls are shingled, and the masonry work is of brick and cement, while a white composition is used for the roof. The main woodwork of the exterior is stained a dark brown, with white trim, and these, together with the red brick, white cement and white roofing, produce an interesting color scheme.

There is a small front porch and a pergola on one side, both of which have cement steps and flooring. In the rear is the usual screened porch with its stationary wash tubs.

The interior is very compact and cozy in its arrangement. The living room, in front, contains a chimneypiece of old-gold brick, with a built-in bookcase on one side and a seat on the other. The top of this seat is

TWO THOUSAND DOLLARS FOR A SIMPLE HOME

CORNER OF DINING ROOM IN THE DREW BUNGALOW, SHOWING PANELED WALLS AND SIMPLE BUILT-IN BUFFET: THERE IS JUST THE SORT OF HOME ATMOSPHERE ONE WOULD EXPECT IN A BUNGALOW OF THIS TYPE.

hinged so that the space underneath may be used as the fuel receptacle. The woodwork, which is of Oregon pine, is given a finish like Flemish oak, and the walls are covered with a paper of soft brown. In this room as well as in the dining room and small library, the flooring is of polished oak.

The dining room opens from the living room and has glass doors leading into the side pergola, in addition to the group of four windows on the right. An attractive and convenient buffet is built at one end, as shown in the photograph. The walls are paneled to a height about four feet six inches, along the top of which is a narrow plate rail. The paper used in this room is olive green, but the woodwork is finished like that of the living room.

There are two bedrooms of ample dimensions, between which the bathroom is placed, and a small hall separates them from the rest of the house. The woodwork in these rooms and in the hall is enameled white, and the walls in the two sleeping rooms have paper of moiré pattern in delicate shades.

The kitchen possesses an unusually complete and practical arrangement of cupboards and other fittings and is of convenient size for a home of this kind. Behind the kitchen is a little breakfast room with a built-in cupboard. White enamel is used for the woodwork of both these rooms, also for the kitchen walls.

As indicated by the view of the dining room, the interior of this bungalow is very simple and homelike. The furnishings are few, but well chosen and the whole arrangement is such as to make the household work light.

The bungalow is the home of Mr. R. H. Drew, of Los Angeles, California, and was designed by E. B. Rust, an architect of that city. Costing but $2,000 in Los Angeles, it should be duplicated for approximately that sum in almost any locality. It does not possess a furnace, however, and this would be needed in other climates. But a furnace for a building of this size should cost less than a hundred dollars—not counting the excavation, which would naturally vary according to local conditions.

Being only 28 feet wide, the bungalow is particularly suitable for a narrow lot, and for this reason as well as for the convenience of its arrangement and economy of its construction, the plan merits careful consideration from those who contemplate the erection of an inexpensive home.

To those who expect to build on a corner lot, and need a design of this simple, economical type, the plan would also appeal, for it could be placed with the living room and porch fronting one street, and the dining room windows overlooking the other, with the bedrooms at the rear for quiet and privacy. If it seemed preferable, in

TWO THOUSAND DOLLARS FOR A SIMPLE HOME

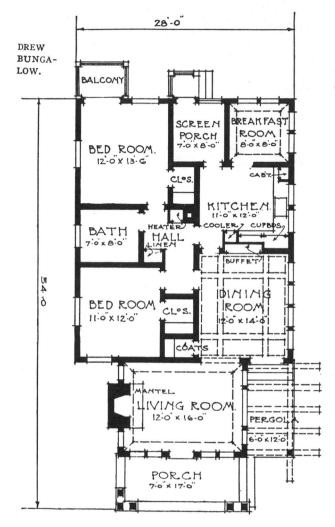

FLOOR PLAN.

such a case, to screen the kitchen and breakfast room more effectually from the street, the pergola which is now indicated in the corner could be projected and extended along the dining room, kitchen and breakfast room wall. This would increase the outdoor living space, screen the bungalow better from the view of passersby, and add considerably to its architectural interest. In order to avoid darkening the kitchen windows, the planting of vines might be omitted at this point.

For a wide but shallow lot, the plan would also be practical, in which case also the pergola arrangement just suggested would be desirable across the front—which is now the side.

Needless to say, a home of this character is equally suited in design, construction and interior arrangement to an Eastern as to a Western site. Indeed, the influence of California architecture is quite noticeable among our modern Eastern bungalows.

"BRIARWOOD": A HILLSIDE HOME AMONG THE TREES

THERE are few sites that lend themselves to home-building with more readiness and charm than a wooded hillside. This is partly because the sloping ground gives an opportunity for that irregularity of architectural contour which is so apt to result in a picturesque air, and partly because the trees, especially if they are evergreens, form a warm, friendly background against which the house seems to nestle, while the foliage and branches in the foreground help to break the lines of the building and give its newness a fairly mellow look.

We are presenting here an unusually attractive little country home of this character, owned by two business women—Dr. Alle Smith and Sue Dorris—and designed by the former. "Briarwood" is the name of this inviting retreat—so-called from the abundance of sweetbriar that grows all around. And the simple design and finish of the building, both inside and out, are quite in keeping with its woodland name.

The winding steps form a pleasant link between hill and home, the porch and balcony offer plenty of space for outdoor living, and the general shape of the cottage with its dormered roof, suggests the simple comfort to be found within. The balcony was especially built to afford an elevated outdoor vantage point from which could be enjoyed the wonderful view presented by

HILLSIDE BUNGALOW OWNED BY TWO BUSINESS WOMEN, DR. ALLE SMITH AND SUE DORRIS: THE BUNGALOW, WHICH WAS DESIGNED BY DR. SMITH, COST ONLY $2,200.

"BRIARWOOD," A HILLSIDE HOME

ONE END OF THE LIVING ROOM SHOWING THE HOME-MADE TILE FIREPLACE PROVIDED WITH WATER COILS THAT SUPPLY RADIATORS IN THREE OTHER ROOMS.

the landscape around the front of the house. And behind the building is a concrete retaining wall, beyond which is the kitchen garden. This wall is covered, in season, with nasturtiums, which give a bright spot of color to the scene.

The outside of the bungalow is covered with rough rustic shingles, stained a driftwood gray, and for the inside trim is used fir of comparatively fine grain, which is given a warm gray stain. The inside walls are tinted the same tone, and the ceilings are a rich cream color. These neutral shades form an excellent background for the hangings, which are blue gray with colored borders in Japanese design. The contrasting colors needed to brighten the rooms are furnished by the Turkish rugs, pottery, Maxfield Parrish pictures and other decorative features. The two photographs of the interior give a general idea of the simplicity with which the place is furnished. There is no crowding of pieces, and everything is planned for use, durability and comfort, the decorative effects being mainly the outcome of homelike arrangement and harmonious design.

The most interesting feature of the living room is, of course, the fireplace, which is built of tiles made by the owners under the instruction of Miss Olive Newcomb, now teacher in the Los Angeles schools. The clay of which these tiles were made was found less than half a mile from the site of the bungalow, so that they literally add a bit of "local color" to the room. They are lightly tinted in harmony with the color scheme of the interior, and on each side, as seen in the picture, is inlaid a panel picture done in clay, made from a camera view taken by Sue Dorris. Above the mantel is a motto in tiles—"East, West, Home's Best"—which completes this much-admired chimneypiece.

But perhaps the most important thing about the fireplace is the fact that it is so constructed as to heat not only the living room but other rooms besides—for, according to the opinion of the two enterprising women who own this charming home, the heating system was much too vital a matter to be disposed of in the usual casual way, by leaving it in the hands of an outsider, however expert. They devised, therefore a system of coils which carry water from the fireplace to the radiators in the various rooms, and then to a reserve tank. There are three radiators in this system—one in the dining room, one in the first-floor bedroom, and another in the dressing room upstairs. The bath is also connected with the fireplace and range, so that there is always plenty of hot water to be had.

"BRIARWOOD," A HILLSIDE HOME

Those who are contemplating the building of a country bungalow may find many helpful suggestions in the two floor plans shown with this article. The main entrance is from the sheltered recessed porch into the long living room with its fireplace, bookshelves and corner seat. Beyond, through the arch, is the dining room with a built-in

A CORNER OF THE CHEERFUL DINING ROOM: A BUILT-IN BUFFET EXTENDS BENEATH THE FARTHER WINDOW.

FLOOR PLAN OF "BRIARWOOD," DESIGNED BY A BUSINESS WOMAN.

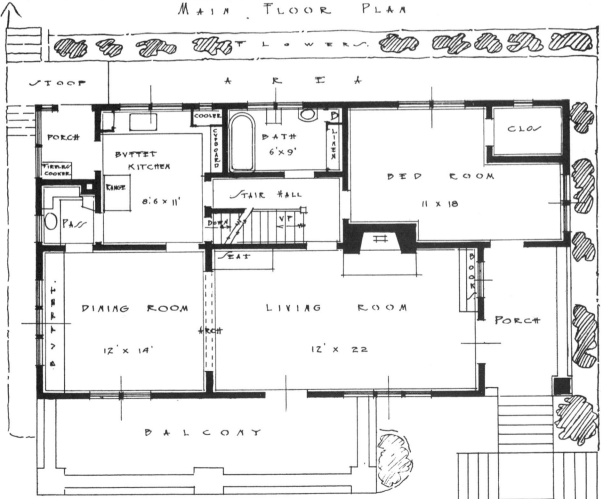

MAIN FLOOR PLAN

"BRIARWOOD," A HILLSIDE HOME

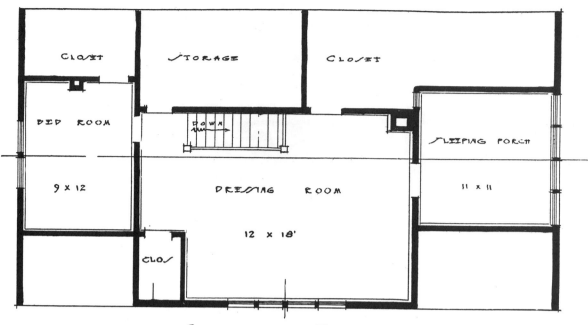

CLOSET STORAGE CLOSET

BED ROOM

DOWN

SLEEPING PORCH

9 X 12

DRESSING   ROOM

11 X 11

CLO/

12 X 18'

SECOND FLOOR

SECOND FLOOR PLAN OF "BRIARWOOD."

buffet occupying the farther end beneath the windows. A small pass pantry leads to the kitchen, which can also be reached through another door, and from one corner of the kitchen the cellar stairs descend beneath the main flight. A glassed-in service porch is provided at the rear, and here is placed the fireless cooker.

The rest of the first floor plan is occupied by the bathroom and bedroom, both opening from the stair hall, while on the floor above is a large dressing room, on one side of which is a bedroom and on the other a sheltered sleeping porch open at one end. The rest of the space beneath the room is utilized for closets and storage.

The cost of construction of this bungalow was $2,200—surely a very reasonable amount for such a comfortable home.

THE "COLONIAL BUNGALOW:" A NEW AND CHARMING VARIATION IN HOME ARCHITECTURE: BY CHARLES ALMA BYERS

Photographs by the Author

THE bungalow, since its introduction into this country a few years ago, by way of California, has enjoyed greater popularity than any other type of home. For it has fulfilled in a simple, homelike and usually inexpensive way the needs of a growing number of American families who desired comfortable modern homes that were roomy, compact and convenient, suited to a democratic mode of existence, and provided with plenty of space of sheltered outdoor life.

While retaining these general characteristics, however, the bungalow has always been more or less influenced by other styles of architecture, and in consequence has been passing through a continuous evolution away from its early American prototype, becoming more and more adapted to the requirements of the country as a whole. Originally it was in this country planned for Southern California only, where the climate is mild throughout the year. But even in this land of perpetual summer, the leading bungalow architects have gradually come to realize the desirability of possessing a durably and warmly constructed home—a home, at least, of far better construction than was the bungalow in the beginning. Hence the more substantial modern developments in this field both in the East and West.

The newest variation of the bungalow type is a combination of the original design with the Colonial cottage, and the result has come to be known as the "Colonial bungalow." It includes the most admirable features of the two styles in a particularly charming manner, and is adaptable to almost any locality. Like the bungalow, it is but one story in height and presents a rather low and rambling appearance. On the other hand, it adheres to the cottage characteristics in that its roof is shingled and its outside walls are covered with resawed weather-boarding, which is painted instead of stained. In pitch of roof and projection of eaves it strikes a happy medium between the two styles, and in structural lines in general it retains an almost equal number of the characteristics of each of the original models. Instead, however, of possessing any suggestion of the usual rustic air of the old-time bungalow, it is of extremely dignified Colonial appearance, and of substantial and warm construction. The arrangement and finish of the interior show a marked leaning toward those of the average bungalow, rather than the Colonial style, which means greater convenience and comfort.

THE "COLONIAL BUNGALOW"

THE accompanying illustrations reveal a particularly successful example of this new style of home, and will be found worth studying by those who contemplate building along these general lines. The house has a frontage of thirty-nine feet and a depth of forty-seven. The siding and all the finishing timbers are painted white, the shingled roof is moss green, and the exposed masonry work is of bluish-red brick. The combination of colors is particularly effective, and the simple mahogany-finished front door gives a touch of contrast that emphasizes the entrance in a pleasant, hospitable manner. Over this door is a slight canopy-like projection, the rest of the front porch being practically an uncovered terrace.

This terrace, as well as the walk and steps leading to it, is of brick, and along the outer edge are placed four garden urns containing dwarfed shrubs, which add an attractive note to the bungalow. There are four French windows in the front wall and three in the wall next to the side street, and those that do not open upon the front terrace are provided with small brick landings that serve also to break up the line of the foundation and link the bungalow with the surrounding grounds. A rather massive outside chimney of brick is a prominent feature of one corner, and it is to the excellence of the masonry throughout that much of the charm of the exterior is due. Every detail, however, has received the most careful attention, even to the arrangement of suitable awnings over the windows.

An especially admirable outside feature of this home is the small court or patio in the rear. Enclosed on three sides, this court provides an excellent outdoor retreat entirely shut off from the view of passersby, and at the same time it receives an unhindered circulation of fresh air. It is floored with cement, and overhead are a few pergola beams which, covered with vines, afford a pleasant shelter from the sun and add considerably to the charm of the court. One French window opens from a rear bedroom into this inviting enclosure, and three others lead from the dining room, the rear wall of which is thus practically of glass.

AS the floor plan shows, the arrangement of the interior is both homelike and convenient. Folding glass doors form the only division between the living room and dining room, and by throwing these wide open the two may be converted into virtually one large room. In the living room is an open fireplace with facing and hearth of chocolate-colored tile, and in the dining room is a charmingly designed and well-built buffet with a china closet at either end. These two rooms have quarter-sawed oak floors, and the woodwork, which is of straight-grain pine, is given a fumed oak

"COLONIAL BUNGALOW" IN LOS ANGELES, THE HOME OF MARION R. GRAY, DESIGNED BY HAROLD BOWLES, ARCHITECT, AND BUILT AT A TOTAL COST OF THIRTY-FIVE HUNDRED DOLLARS.

DETAIL SHOWING THE PERGOLA-COVERED COURT IN THE REAR OF THE COLONIAL BUNGALOW, WITH FRENCH WINDOWS OPENING FROM THE DINING ROOM: A CHARMING PLACE FOR SERVING MEALS AND FOR GENERAL OUTDOOR LIVING.

FIREPLACE CORNER IN LIVING ROOM OF COLONIAL BUNGALOW
SHOWING TILED MANTEL, SIMPLE SUBSTANTIAL FURNISHINGS
AND TASTEFUL CRETONNE DRAPERIES AT THE LONG WINDOWS.

THE DINING ROOM OF THE BUNGALOW, WITH ITS BUILT-IN
SIDEBOARD AND CHINA CLOSETS, EXCELLENT IN BOTH DESIGN
AND WORKMANSHIP.

THE "COLONIAL BUNGALOW"

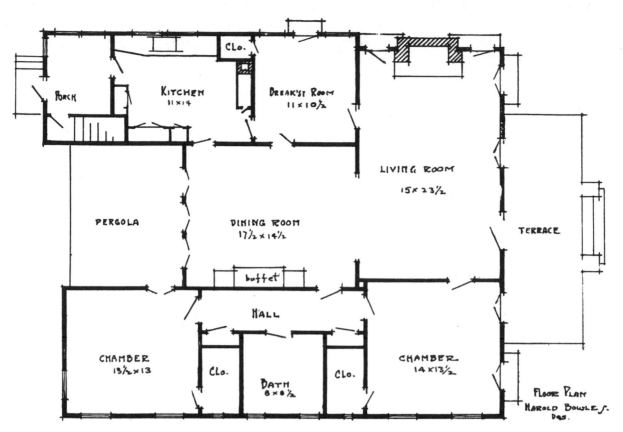

finish. The walls of the dining room are finished with a leatherette wainscot reaching to the usual plate shelf, and the walls above, as in the living room, are papered. The lighting fixtures consist of inverted domes, and the drapery used for the several French windows is yellow-flowered cretonne. The furnishings are simple, substantial and homelike.

On one side of the house, shut away from the living and dining rooms, are the bedrooms and bath. Each of the bedrooms has a roomy closet lighted by a small window, and in the hall that connects these rooms with the bathroom are two small linen closets. The bathroom is finished with a tile wainscot, and the walls of the bedrooms are papered. The woodwork in all of these rooms, as well as in the connecting hall, is enameled white.

The kitchen, which is on the opposite side of the bungalow, possesses all of the usual conveniences, including cupboards, cabinets, drawers, a draught cooler and a hood for the range; and

the finish here also is white enamel. In the rear of the kitchen is the customary screened porch, and between the kitchen and the living room is located the breakfast room, with white enamel woodwork and decorations in delft blue. This room would be equally appropriate for den, library or maid's room.

Under the rear of the house is a basement, eleven by fourteen feet, which is walled and floored with concrete. A hot-air furnace located here furnishes heat to the rooms when required. The stairway to this basement descends from the screened porch behind the kitchen.

This charming and practical little "Colonial bungalow" is located in Los Angeles, California, and is the home of Marion R. Gray. It was designed and built by Harold Bowles, an architect of that city, and represents a total cost of thirty-five hundred dollars. For approximately this sum it should be satisfactorily duplicated in almost any locality.

MAKING THE BUNGALOW EXTERNALLY ATTRACTIVE: BY M. ROBERTS CONOVER

THOUGH the name bungalow comes from India and belongs properly to a one story building consisting of a central large hall with smaller rooms opening from it and a wide covered porch all around to protect from tropical suns, it has come to be quite generally applied in America to almost any small country house. A country house of a story and a half or even two stories if it has a large porch across one or more sides of it is now, though technically incorrect, referred to as a bungalow. In India the name is given to even very large and imposing houses of stone or brick, almost equaling a palace in rank if but one story in height, to government rest houses and to army quarters providing they are but the one story height.

So many of our little country houses are called bungalows that the name has come to be endeared to us. It conjures a comfortable, well shaped little house in the midst of a garden, shaded by trees, with the perfume of flowers floating in through open windows.

It is not difficult to make this picture a reality. The planting of a few vines to give it relation to the garden, a shrub or so at the corners to soften sharp angles and break too severe lines and a tree to give play of light and shade over the house will bring it about. There is a wide list of vines, annuals, perennials, shrubs and ornamental trees from which one may make choice, but several things should be borne in mind; chief of these is the winter aspect of the bungalow. Summer sees to it that it is attractive from April to November, but we must look to it that it is beautiful the rest of the time. There are evergreen shrubs such as pines, cedars, spruces, retinosporas, cypresses that can be had tall or round, dwarfed or large and of many shades of green, and there are the broad leaved shrubs such as

azaleas, laurels, rhododendrons, etc., that in addition to keeping green all winter put forth gorgeous blossoms in the spring and early summer. Many trees are as beautiful in winter as in summer, because of their delicate tracery of branches. Some shrubs have brightly colored stems which after the leaves have fallen give a grateful sense of color. Others like barberries and viburnums have bright berries; so with a little study winter beauty can easily be provided.

For summer planting color harmony must be considered when the main planting of perennials has been decided upon. Then the annuals can be varied with each season. Some of the most ornamental trees are those which bear fruit. Fruit trees in the front yard are not considered proper by some, but no tree takes on a more picturesque form than an old apple or cherry tree. The accompanying photographs hold helpful suggestions for bringing about external beauty of country cottages.

The first photograph shows a bungalow built to give a view of the Raritan Bay through the porch, so that a picture of the bay and sky is had as one approaches the house, which is built on a side hill. The back portion does not resemble a bungalow so much as the front, for it is on a level with the ground. This porch extends around the two sides of this house and forms the main living room of the family during the summer.

The second photograph illustrates the charm of roof and porch lines broken by

BUNGALOW BUILT TO GIVE VIEW OF THE RARITAN BAY FROM THE PORCH.

INTERESTING BUNGALOW ARCHITECTURE

BUNGALOW WITH A LARGE PORCH USED FOR OUTDOOR SITTING ROOM.

the use of a gable. The large tree makes a pleasant play of sunshine and shadow across the house and the large porch suggests a cozy comfortable outdoor room.

The charm of the vine-clad cottage is shown in the third photograph. This cottage is completely covered with Boston ivy. The effect is cool and bowerlike. We can imagine the beauty of color of this house in the fall.

In the fourth photograph an example of planting to cover a basement made conspicuous by the slope of land is given. From the street this house is apparently a one story bungalow. The problem was to cover the necessary and useful basement at the back

of the house formed by the lay of the land. As may be seen it was effectively solved by a planting of blossoming shrubs. The vine against the chimney carries the line on up most gracefully and the trees bear promise of welcome fruit.

The fifth picture shows a bungalow enclosed with boards which are allowed to project log-cabin fashion at the corners. The small windmill is a novel feature for a bungalow. The vines across the front of it make a graceful curtain to shut out too strong rays of the sun. The very simple rustic pergola leading to the front door gives promise of a beautiful walk when the vines have had a chance to cover them.

The last photograph shows how a roof line may be softened in imitation of the old thatched roofs of English cottages. The hedge and the winter trees give promise of summer beauty. An evergreen at either side of the steps and a planting of large leaved evergreens at the corner of the

COOL AND BOWER-LIKE EFFECT OF BUNGALOW COVERED WITH VINES.

INTERESTING EXAMPLE OF PLANTING TO COVER A CONSPICUOUS BASEMENT.

house would have added warmth to this cottage through the long winter.

The economical aspect of artistic building has been commented upon in the most convincing way by Maurice B. Adams. He says, "The artistic aspect of country-side architecture naturally appeals to the majority of readers far more directly than any discussion on financial matters would do, however appropriate and necessary others will consider such a question of ways and means. These last-named essentials frequently induce some to believe that ugly, crude, or tasteless buildings are necessarily cheaper, or that picturesque, convenient, and architecturally well-proportioned buildings must relatively be more costly. This is not true. There is such a thing in building as 'cheap and nasty,' which in plain terms reads 'dear at any price.' Indifferent construction and poor materials will without a doubt incur perpetual expense in the upkeep which bad work always renders unavoidable. There is only one reliable way of minimizing the ultimate cost of maintenance, and if this does mean a larger initial outlay, the advantage of a wise investment is thereby ensured. This self-evident commonplace might perhaps have demanded an apology but for the fact that people are continually endeavoring to obtain what they term 'cheap building work,' and with this end in view are induced to put their faith in the so-called 'practical man,' who, however efficient he may be otherwise, unblushingly gives the most con-

A BUNGALOW ENCLOSED WITH BOARDS WHICH ARE ALLOWED TO PROJECT LOG-CABIN FASHION AT THE CORNERS.

INTERESTING BUNGALOW ARCHITECTURE

THE ROOF LINE OF THIS BUNGALOW IS MADE IN IMITATION OF THATCHED ROOFED ENGLISH COTTAGES.

clusive evidence as to his entire inability to produce well-contrived, properly-built, homely, or tasteful houses. The speculating builder is no doubt often exceedingly clever, and in an ingenious fashion knows how to cater for the public, occasionally providing quite a remarkable amount of accommodation, of a kind, for a strictly modest rental; and he also quite understands to what extent a degree of pretentiousness attracts the popular fancy. He builds to sell, and in common with all speculating investments when he realizes, the profits are large. No architect can compete on these lines with such builders, and he need not attempt to do so. In the long run there can remain no question as to which kind of building pays the owner best. An unqualified designer not only fails to obtain a homely character and graceful simplicity in his work, but he seldom if ever employs his materials economically, scamp as he may; and buildings carried out in this fashion will cost the building owner much more than if he had given his commission to a good architect. Even assuming that the money outlay in either instance be the same, and that in structural stability there is not much difference, it cannot be pretended that the results in any sense are identical, even though the areas of the rooms correspond.

"The main essentials consist of the charm of artistic fitness by which alone a building can be harmonized with its site and surroundings, making it as it were part of the ground on which it stands, restful and unobtrusive, comfortable and suitable. These are the qualities which alone can impart interest and give durable pleasure. Such qualities do not depend so much upon money expenditure as upon an application of thought and good taste. They exist quite apart from elaborateness of detail, and are mostly obtained by avoiding all ornamental excrescences, which ill accord with the environment of the hedgerow and the coppice. Picturesqueness comes of simplicity of form, and belongs to good proportion producing pleasant groupings, giving graceful sky-lines, and casting telling shadows, so essential for contrast and color."

We might add that the picturesqueness that comes of simplicity does not come from the simplicity that is uncouthness, plainness, an unthought-out, unadorned crude thing. True simplicity, the highest attainment of art, approaches the divine. Simplicity does not mean a half formed, ignorant construction, but something so fine, pure and superior that it stands apart from the ordinary as a flower stands apart from common weeds.

A STORY OF HOME-MAKING

(Illustrated by photographs of a house designed by J. S. Long, and built by the Long Building Co.)

WHEN one enters upon the pleasant adventure of home making, all sorts of exciting things begin to happen, as is quite to be expected with adventures. The most carefully laid plans fail utterly and better ones arise in their stead, disappointment over the result of some detail is soon forgotten in success beyond all hope of another one. But unlike Stevenson's joy of the road that was so much greater than the "arriving," the quest of the home, joyous though it is, cannot compare with the quiet hours of peace and contentment after the home is finished and one looks upon his work and sees that it is good. It is good to sit upon one's own vine-covered porch and contemplate the many perfections of the hard won achievement, to enjoy in retrospect the paths of difficulty and of pleasure over which the adventure led.

The story of home making ought to be as interesting as any other tale of adventure, of travels in a new land or even of love, for every home story is the best kind of a love story. A house is much like a composite picture—designers, carpenters, masons, plumbers, brick, mortar, steel and wood, furniture and furnishings of silk, cotton, linen, glassware,

HOUSE ALONG CRAFTSMAN LINES, DESIGNED AND BUILT BY THE LONG BUILDING CO., SEATTLE.

tin and silver have all influenced the character of the finished house, left some weak or strong, beautiful or ugly impress of themselves upon the final picture. Houses are recorders of experience, vouchers of taste or the lack of it. A man's thumb-prints upon paper have no more convicting a variation of individuality than the house he elects to build upon the lot of his choice. The bumps and depressions of a man's head are no more an indication of his character than the windows, porches, roof and doors of his house— were there some new species of phrenologist to interpret them. The preference of Georgian, Colonial, Dutch, English, Craftsman or the many other styles are as

LIVING ROOM SHOWING FIREPLACE NOOK IN THIS SAME HOUSE.

A STORY OF HOME-MAKING

DINING ROOM OF THE HOUSE DESIGNED BY THE LONG BUILDING CO.

indicative of temperament as the choice of one's clothing.

Every mail brings us some pleasant report of homes built along Craftsman lines, because there was something in them that found echo in the hearts of the builders, some note of sympathy, some expression of practicality, some demand for honesty.

Mr. J. S. Long has recently sent us the floor plans and photographs of a bungalow designed by him, one, as he says, "in distinctly Craftsman style." This house, though designed especially for a corner lot, can just as well be built on any 60 foot lot.

The following detailed description will certainly be appreciated by prospective builders who desire a house of this size. It is of cedar shingles laid two, three and seven inches to the weather and all exterior trim with the exception of window and door panes is of selected rough fir. The main body of the house is stained a light brown, the rough trim a little darker. The roof is black; window and door frames, sash and lattice on rear porch are pure white; with this rustic texture and color, cobblestones are undoubtedly the most effective material of which a chimney could be made. Concrete would have made too extreme a contrast, dark clinker-brick might have been used, but the cobblestones, especially since a few stones appear in the garden, seem perfectly appropriate. Vines will in time add to the rustic naturalness of the whole effect.

From the pergola porch at the side of the house, an excellent view of Mount Ranier can be obtained and from the front porch Lake Washington and the Cascades may be seen. With such superb triumphs of nature as neighbors, it would seem sacrilege to intrude a too ornate, artificial, flippantly designed house. The site demands an unobtrusive, respectful, harmonious structure with windows and porches, permitting the beauty of nature to be enjoyed in the ever changing aspects of morning and evening light. A certain reverent simple dignity of architecture is fitting.

Within, this house was ordered for comfort and convenience of housekeeping. A study of the floor plans reveals that thought

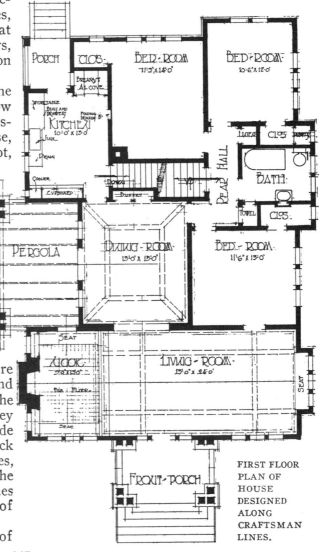

FIRST FLOOR PLAN OF HOUSE DESIGNED ALONG CRAFTSMAN LINES.

A STORY OF HOME-MAKING

PULLMAN DINING ALCOVE, FOLDING IRONING BOARD
CLOSET SHOWN BY THE GAS STOVE.

dining room is beamed and paneled and a buffet built in the side nearest the kitchen. The woodwork gives a soft warm glow to the room. Absence of all gingerbread work gives it a pleasant, modest dignity.

But it is in the kitchen that the greatest ingenuity has been displayed. This room is what the Long Building Company, architects and builders, declare to be a "strictly cabinet" kitchen throughout, that is, it is arranged to save unnecessary steps, planned with every thought for the minimizing of labor, with every care for convenience, with the ideal of intensive housekeeping always in mind. Everything has been placed within easy reach for the work at hand; a stairway leads directly from the kitchen to

has been taken to make the interior seem as open and roomy as possible, to save steps in the kitchen, to get bedrooms and baths conveniently related. How many home ideas have been incorporated within the compass of that small home! The vine-wreathed porch for pleasing entrance, the cozy fireplace flanked by shelves of books, the sunny dining room with pergola hard by that can be incorporated with it in one glorious room simply by opening wide the glass doors, the outdoor pergola that can be sitting room or breakfast room as needed, the kitchen, with all that heart can desire in the way of cupboards, spacious bedrooms, large attic storage place and healthful sleeping porch, all go toward the making of a most delightful and convenient home.

The living room and tile fireplace-nook together make a room 33 feet in length. By raising the "cozy nook" up from the main room by two steps a little sense of privacy or of importance was given it. On either side of this reading or conversation corner are seats hinged so that they provide convenient storage space. The cove pointed granite fireplace extends to the ceiling. Opposite this rest end of the room is a bay window with a built-in seat. The walls are paneled and the ceiling is beamed. All the woodwork here and in the dining room has been stained a mission brown and the walls kalsomined to a creamy tint that suitably corresponds with it. The

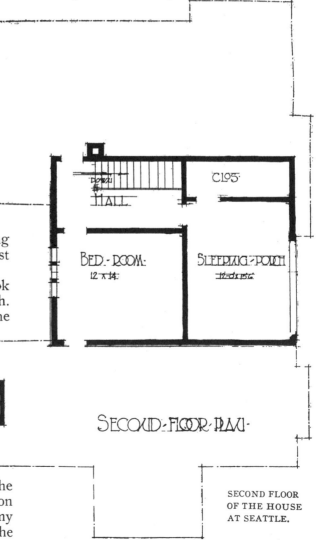

SECOND-FLOOR-PLAN·

SECOND FLOOR
OF THE HOUSE
AT SEATTLE.

the large cement basement in which are located the coal bins, fruit room and laundry. There are a number of clever built-in features, such as a folding ironing board, flour bins, coolers, drawers, work table and cupboards, the latter being located in the wall nearest the dining room. One of the most practical features is the "Pullman" breakfast alcove. Every home maker who prepares her own meals will appreciate the saving of labor which such an alcove provides. It saves many a trip in and out of the dining room, with first the dishes and the food, with many return trips to the kitchen, after the meal is over and the putting in order of the dining room. Such an arrangement is a great labor saver, and with its flower shelf and cozy relation to the attractive kitchen it certainly is a pleasant place in which to have breakfast. Everyone likes a kitchen if it is well ordered. Under a home-loving woman's efficient management it is often the pleasantest room in the house, a room where every member of the family so loves to congregate that they get "underfoot" in most obstructive way.

Three bedrooms, each with ample, well lighted closets, and a bath, are provided on the first floor, while an additional bedroom and large sleeping porch are located upstairs. All these rooms are finished in enameled old ivory. It will be observed that there is an abundance of light in each room and also a window in each closet. For a house of this size there is little left to be desired in the way of cheerful home comfort; but the best thing about it all is the amazingly low cost of its building. The figures which we give below seem to cover a great deal of good material and work for very little money. We are publishing the full cost of this fine little home just as a proof of what can be done under skilled planning, management and careful oversight: Excavating, $45; concrete walls, $230; concrete floor, $110; brick, $150; tile, $50; lumber and mill work, $900; hardwood, $90; hardware, $85; sheet metal, $25; plastering $185; plumbing, $200; sewer, $45; carpenter work, $500; electric light wiring, $70; furnace heat, $140; painting, $175; miscellaneous, $50; ground, $300; total, $3,350. These figures of course represent what can be done in the West and not in the East. However, though some items would be greater in the East, some others would be less.

A CHARMING SIMPLE BUNGALOW WITH PALATIAL FURNISHINGS: BY CHARLES ALMA BYERS

Photographs by Lenwood Abbott.

A CHARMING bungalow home in Southern California embowered in flowers and greenery throughout the year is outlined, sometimes bathed in purple haze, against a wall of mountains. In the valley below it is always summer, but the peaks of the mountain wall often wear a crown of snow. Near the bungalow grow stately eucalypti and straggly oaks, the bungalow itself is low and rambling, and from whatever point it is viewed it conveys a most picturesque impression.

And even more interesting, but in a different way, is its interior. Ordinarily one thinks of the bungalow as a type of home adaptable only to the tastes of the family of moderate means. But the bungalow we are showing in this article is the home of a millionaire, and its interior is palatial in its furnishings and decorations. There are rare old pieces of furniture, antique mirrors, paintings by old masters, and rich rugs and draperies from many lands, while among the collection of books are found volumes of almost priceless value. Certainly one would rarely ever find a home of more elegance.

THE OPEN END OF THE PATIO IS SCREENED BY A ROW OF BAY TREES. HOME OF JOHN P. CUDAHY, ESQ.

Structurally, this bungalow is an excellent representation of the popular bungalow home of California. It is designed to enclose an open court or *patio,* on three sides. In the main it is but a single story high, but one of the wings possesses a low second-floor addition. The shingled roof is of comparatively slight pitch and has wide overhangs in the eaves and gables. The walls of the first-floor portion are of creamy white stucco over building tile, while the walls of the upper part are covered with redwood shakes. The woodwork is stained a soft brown color, which contrasts strikingly with the creamy stucco, and produces a very attractive color scheme.

Perhaps the most generally admired feature of the bungalow, structurally, is the *patio.* It is roomy and airy, and with decorative lattice work covering the walls. It is floored with dark red brick, and overhead it is entirely unprotected, save for the wide projections of the roof. A row of bay trees screens it on the open side, and from one of the rear corners a tall picturesque old eucalyptus grows right up through the flooring. To even more closely link this *patio* with the extensive garden plot which surrounds the house, a number of palms and ferns spring from aptly placed fern boxes and jardinieres of rare old terra cotta from Venice. Much

A SIMPLE BUNGALOW, RICHLY FURNISHED

of the floor space is carpeted with weatherproof rugs, and wicker chairs and tables furnish it.

Besides this *patio* there is a pergola-veranda along the side of one of the wings. This is likewise paved with brick, and pergola beams are the only covering. A low perpendicular-boarded parapet, coped with a continuous flower box, forms the outside enclosure, and into the space open two sets of French doors, making it another convenient and inviting retreat.

ENTERING the house through this pergola, one is ushered directly into the immense drawing room, which is over forty feet in length. To maintain the bungalow appearance here, the rafters and braces are exposed, but in every other respect one might imagine that he had stepped into a palace. Papal velvet hangings of deep red are at the doors and windows, and the Papal lamps of copper are swung by chains from the old Saxon crown design; the high-backed chairs, the carved tables of English oak and the wonderful old screen from a French chateau combine to give the impression of England in the time of King Richard the Lion Hearted. This old early English idea is still further emphasized by the antique church bench which has been cushioned in velvet, the odd fender rail in front of the fireplace, and by the pictures and

BUNGALOW IN PASADENA, CALIFORNIA, DESIGNED FOR JOHN P. CUDAHY, ESQ., MYRON HUNT, ARCHITECT.

antique mirrors which grace the walls. Oriental rugs cover the floor, and in the center is a square of rich red, like the velvet hangings at the doors and windows. Along a portion of one of the side walls is an immense case full of books—plain books in wonderful bindings and wonderful books in plain bindings. Many of them are very old and rare, among them a set of Shakespeare printed in 1830.

At right angles to the long drawing room is the dining room, with only the velvet hangings intervening, and here again one gets a fine sense of perspective, for it is fifty-five feet from one end of the dining room across the end of the drawing room. The walls of this room are in old blue, gold and copper tones, and the velvet hangings are of Gobelin blue; the furniture is Jacobean with the high-backed chairs cushioned in blue.

The music room is reminiscent of France, with its pale gold covered walls, its hangings of soft champagne tone. There is a fireplace in one corner of the room, and before it is a French firescreen. The mahogany chairs are covered in embroidered gold brocade, and the lighting fixture is a chandelier of carved wood from Florence, which has been treated with dull gold.

Adjoining the music room is a boudoir,

A SIMPLE BUNGALOW, RICHLY FURNISHED

which is finished in delicate shades of pink and rose. Pink satin covers the walls, and in one corner is a huge pink covered couch. The chairs are covered in rose, as is a small sewing table.

The house also contains a children's sunny nursery, a den, and sleeping porch.

PATIO WITH LATTICE WORK COVERING WALLS, FLOORED WITH DARK RED BRICK.

This unusual bungalow is located in Pasadena, California, and is the home of Mr. and Mrs. John P. Cudahy. It was designed by Myron Hunt, a well known California architect.

DRAWING ROOM OF THE CUDAHY HOME SHOWING SHELVES FILLED WITH RARE OLD BOOKS.